31 DAYS TO
MILLIONAIRE
MARKETING
MIRACLES

31 DAYS TO MILLIONAIRE MARKETING MIRACLES

ATTRACT MORE LEADS, GET MORE CLIENTS, AND MAKE MORE SALES

TRACY REPCHUK

WILEY

Published by John Wiley & Sons, Inc., Hoboken, New Jersey.
Published simultaneously in Canada.

For general information about our other products and services, please contact our Customer Care Department within the United States at (800) 762-2974, outside the United States at (317) 572-3993 or fax (317) 572-4002.

Wiley publishes in a variety of print and electronic formats and by print-on-demand. Some material included with standard print versions of this book may not be included in e-books or in print-on-demand. If this book refers to media such as a CD or DVD that is not included in the version you purchased, you may download this material at http://booksupport.wiley.com. For more information about Wiley products, visit www.wiley.com.

Library of Congress Cataloging-in-Publication Data

Repchuk, Tracy Lynn.
    31 days to millionaire marketing miracles : attract more leads, get more clients, and make more sales / Tracy Repchuk.
      pages cm
    Includes bibliographical references and index.
    ISBN 978-1-118-68441-2 (pbk.); ISBN 978-1-118-74225-9 (ebk);
    ISBN 978-1-118-74230-3 (ebk)
      1. Marketing. 2. Strategic planning. 3. Internet marketing. I. Title. II. Title:
    Thirty one days to millionaire marketing miracles.
    HF5415.R437 2013
    658.8—dc23

                                                                      2013016036

Printed in the United States of America

10 9 8 7 6 5 4 3 2 1

CONTENTS

FOREWORD

As a promoter and founder of the World Internet Summit (WIS), I meet thousands of newcomers to Internet marketing every year. From this I have begun to recognize quickly the ones that will take action and apply what they learn, and even Tracy Repchuk surpassed those expectations.

Within the first five months she had already made $95,717, had more than 3,000 subscribers, and released a book to best-seller status from start to finish in 58 days; as a result, WIS flew her to Singapore to appear on stage as the "New Success of the Year" at the World Internet Mega Summit.

In the weeks after, she was already booked to appear at a UK show with her own product line and coaching program. Her title has become Marketing Makeover Maestro, as she has an incredible ability to take information and transform it into simple terms that allow anyone access to how to become a success using Internet marketing. She has a particular appeal to the female demographic and the newbies who want to succeed at the rate she has, which is now labeled a *Quantum Leap*.

I knew right away that she was a force to admire, and quickly invited her to speak around the world with the World Internet Summit organization. This book is a wonderful reflection of the care she takes to present a business approach to Internet marketing, combined with the reality of this abundant field.

It is my honor to be a part of this project, and I encourage you to follow her advice and combine the power of your passion with the provided resources to move you beyond just reading into dream-producing action.

—Brett McFall
Co-Founder of the World Internet Summit Organization

ACKNOWLEDGMENTS

This book, although written completely by myself, could not have happened without the support and love of my amazing husband, Dave, and my three children: Kennedy, Celeste, and Caleb.

I thank all of the mentors who were and are a part of my continuing journey to always do better, help more people, and give more back.

And finally, a special thanks to my parents, Harold and Margaret Broadbent; without them, none of this would have been possible.

PREFACE

To keep up with trends and the ever changing landscape of the Internet, this book is now on its 10th edition, serving as the go-to reference guide and blueprint for the Internet marketing industry. What I teach you is exactly what I did to create an Internet marketing empire—from *one* idea—and it all started with this book, which is now the cornerstone to my successful business. The industry changes a lot every year, but what I love still is that the foundation remains the same. That is what you are about to learn. I discuss the current trends that are working; and throughout the book I keep the staple elements in place while integrating all of the new trends you need to know about.

INTRODUCTION

Do Not Skip This Section

INTERNET MARKETING CAN BE A LONELY PLACE

When I think of Internet marketing I have flashbacks of the hit TV show *Seinfeld* where Jerry was wildly successful and even though his blundering gang was a part of the "club," they lived vicariously attempting to make life work in their favor. In most cases they ended up living off Jerry's scraps or generosity. Even more hopeful was Newman. He was an integral component to the diverse mix of characters, but survived as an outcast, often envious and yearning to be even a small part of this elusive lifestyle.

Internet marketing can be a lot like that. Chances are you have felt like a Newman at some point (or maybe even still do)— just on the outskirts of having it all. Not yet part of the club. Yearning for just one sweet drop of that camaraderie and success, enough just to give you hope that the path you have chosen will not leave you about to crash and burn like Newman's postal truck on a carefree drive down the Internet marketing highway.

At this point it is important to remember that it may feel like you are not a part of the Internet marketing community when you first start out, but at each step you do move closer to your ultimate dreams. You will discover that the club will not always feel exclusive, and that there are just different levels of membership. You go from being a new member and buying products and services, to the point where you have made a fortune by developing or mastering one of the many formulas to become your own Internet marketing success. Then, you are really in.

Once you understand that you play a big role in a hierarchy of guru status success right from the beginning, you will see that it is part of a cycle, and it will one day be your turn to exchange your product in abundance, and be at the other end of your next level of membership.

So why then is it a lonely place? Because while you are trying to figure it out, decipher the codes, tap into the secrets, apply them, buy them, and generally pig out on the information smorgasbord, there is not much two-way communication. The communication is done with autoresponders or teleseminars, where they are talking to you but not with you. Many times you sit on the other end with a question dripping hungrily from your information-splattered chin and have to turn to your only friend—Google or Yahoo. There you start a journey of investigations that either leads you to a treasure of insightful delights, or a black hole of chaos where the vortex pull is so strong you forgot why you even journeyed into the inner depths of the World Wide Web to begin with.

SEARCHING FOR "THE ONE"

This leaves you in a precarious place. Sure there are many people out there who have pioneered through the vast landscape and managed to discover their pot of gold, but what about the rest? Are they destined to roam the lands, hungry, thirsty, wiping sweat from their experience-stained brows, only to end up empty-handed once again?

Well, that is entirely up to you.

THE TSUNAMI OF LIFE

When you first get started with all of your enthusiasm, sometimes the road will not be straight. I was hit with a tsunami that tried to rip my dreams out of my clenched hands. I started my first company while I was still in college at the age of 19, in 1985. Together with my college boyfriend, we planned our life together. We were incredibly successful as custom software developers with a line of our own software products around the world. I had further studied to secure a Certified Management Accountants designation, and a seat on the CMA Provincial Board of Governors where I was the youngest ever elected, which combined provided me with my BMW, Mercedes, Jeep, country estate, multiple homes, vacation properties, and a completely carefree life by the time I hit the ripe old age of 24.

Then, we got engaged, but it's not the happily-ever-after ending you might be thinking, because two weeks before the wedding, he called it off. He was with someone else, and then she got pregnant and he was going to marry her. I had to work side-by-side with him through agony and heartache, and watched him with her, while I still loved him. The pain did not stop there, for I did something foolish—and that was to pick someone who was clearly not right for me. Then, yes, in June of 1989, we got married, while I was still reeling from this original devastation.

That is where my problems began, because within a short time of being married it was not as Martha Stewart would say, "A Good Thing." It took me almost four years to get a divorce, cost me thousands and thousands as he fought for every ounce that he could get out of me, emptied our personal bank account, emptied the house of the furniture while I was at work (he was still a student at university when I met him), and then he came after my company. But, that wasn't the hard part. It all came tumbling down on me with the full fury of a tsunami when during all of this, running a company, watching my ex-fiancé with his new wife and daughter, the wife decided she wanted me away from her husband and out of the company. Immediately the locks to my business were changed, business credit cards were cut off, and I was locked out of my business and my home. I had two men vying for my company at the same time, and stripping me of everything I had built. What was I to do?

After months of trying to determine what my ex-fiancé had done to the company that he needed me to stay away, I discovered that it was $100,000 in debt and still owed almost $200,000 in deliverable custom programming projects, most of which all the money had been collected for and no work had been done. Now what? I got a loan for $80,000 and bought him out. I brought in a partner, who has now been my husband for 17 years, and we pulled that company out of bankruptcy, restored our credit, delivered all of the projects with no funding to pay for them, and started again. What did my ex-partner do? He moved directly across the street, started a business doing the same thing, and stole all of my staff.

So What Is the Moral of That Story?

I could have done many things. I could have curled into a ball in the fetal position and waited for time to heal all wounds. I could have walked away from the company, my mortgage, and what I had built. Declared bankruptcy, started all over again—fresh. I could have said, "but he was the one that got away" and never moved on with my life. Like I said, though, the road of life won't be straight and I knew even back then the power of my thoughts so I thought, "What do I need to do to fix this?"

YOU NEVER KNOW WHAT'S AROUND THE NEXT CORNER

When you ask yourself big questions, they get answered, but you have to be able to hear them. My answer came when I discovered a bookstore with a wall of books that spanned the whole length of the store. It was so enormous that it had to represent a significant discovery of our time, and that led me to the fix—being a very early adopter of the World Wide Web.

During my decade of using the Internet as a brochure for my company, I started to delve more deeply into the online swirl and quickly turned into a full-fledged mentee. A mentee is someone who seeks out the guidance of a person who has more experience in a certain area, called a mentor, and I knew I needed one. Even with a string of mentors and a background in web development and SEO (search engine optimization), a piece of the puzzle was always missing, which was what would cause a flow of money in an automated fashion—the promise I was constantly hearing. This caused me to study exactly what successful companies were doing, because I had no doubt at all they were making piles of cash, but there was something missing in translation. Finally, after evaluating the data flow from what they were doing to the big money part, I discovered there was a foundation or path they followed. Without having this in place, there was a gap in understanding and ability to convert an idea to an Internet marketing empire, and they were so beyond this part there was an assumption that this already existed for everyone. This book reiterates what they are doing, and, in turn, what I did to make it work, in a language and sequence I hope provides you the missing link.

You will discover the steps and sequence required to turn your passions into profits with benefits such as:

- How to avoid the #1 mistake most new Internet seekers make.

- Discover Quantum Leap Thinking and the Millionaire Mind-Set you need to succeed.

- Experience a "31-Point Marketing Makeover Miracle" blueprint created from the testing and combination of the most brilliant Internet programs out there.

- Secrets about the three websites you need to market your vision and build your brand.

- Create your own big picture marketing technique that keeps you focused.

- Master Rapid Product Creation in five easy steps.

- Proven Joint Venture Basics that get results.

- Blogging essentials for monetizing your site.

- Deadly website combos that skyrocket your profits.

- Autoresponder secrets that will cause your subscribers to buy.

- Top visitor capture techniques you must have.

- Understand Market Funnel marketing for big buck profits . . . and much, much more!

MOTIVATIONS COME FROM FUNNY PLACES

This book started with the fact that each year I make a New Year's resolution to lose weight but this year I decided to do something different. On January 1, 2007, I decided to take the resolution concept and spend 31 days posting a complete plan to my blog so that everyone could apply it, and make this the year of financial freedom. Instead of losing the weight, it was time to teach others how to gain wealth.

31 Days to Millionaire Marketing Miracles became "The diet that never was." I pieced together a blueprint of all the elements I had implemented that worked, and notified the subscribers of my ezine of the journey we were about to take.

It seemed fitting to start at the beginning because it is where most of the newbies start. From my blog, I had people contacting me thanking me for posting this, and saying it was really helpful, and it was just what they needed. I made $5,497 on my second day by taking my offline skills (direct sales copywriting) and moving it online into Landing Pages. I detected this was something that was definitely needed and wanted from that reaction.

Although I have not come up with some revolutionary new way of marketing, or formula, or concept, I do make my living by following what works. I have tried many programs, made many mistakes, got many to work, got ripped off by some, and managed at the very least to put together the big picture as a feat of organization.

This is the 10th edition and 14th version of this book as I continue to check all links and ensure that new technology gets updated. In addition, as I write this version I am a stable part of the Internet marketing community. It has been a testament to the accuracy of the data in the book, and what I teach. I do not teach what I have not tried and I do not pass on to you what does not work. In addition, I am now the #1 Woman Speaker in the World for Internet Marketing, and appear on the same stages as the mentors' names I put on the pedestal in the beginning. I have traveled to more than 37 countries and have appeared with almost every big name including Joe Sugarman, Mark Joyner, Mike Filsaime, Joel Comm, Robert Allen, Joel Bauer, Dave Lakhani, Armand Morin, Kevin Harrington (ABC's *Shark Tank*), and the list goes on. I have moved away primarily now from the multispeaker stages to my own events/stages, but once in a while I accept one if the promoter is a friend or making the type of impact I support. I have traveled the distance of going around the world seven times, to appearing on my own stages. I have taken hundreds of clients through my mentor programs and thousands through my products and clubs.

This book shows you how to build the foundation of your business by using Internet marketing, and presents how to go about it in an easy step-by-step plan. My purpose is to have you read this and know the steps to take, the people to get in touch with, the programs to investigate, so you know what you have to do. I want you to have something working where you are at least starting to hit the first tier of your "celebrate your victories" chart. Then you can start to work the plan, and achieve the ultimate dreams: "Make Money While You Sleep" and "Live the Freedom Lifestyle." You do this by getting the steps in place, and repeating them over and over, making it a 31-day plan. All you have to do is be a researcher, an implementer, and a risk taker. I did not originate this material. I translated what I learned from many, many mentors, tested it, and put it into a sequence you can understand and follow.

Quantum Leap Thinking

If I learned anything from following the yellow brick road, it's that when you take the time to do something right, life moves faster because you do not have to leap over gaping holes, crawl over barriers, and constantly go back to fix stuff you missed. From my entry into the Internet marketing world I started to be called a *Quantum Leap Expert*. A Quantum Leap is when something happens faster than anyone thought possible, and really does not seem to follow any conventions of logic. For example, this book went from concept, to being written, to best seller in 58 days. In five months I had made more money than most do in a year, certainly more than I even did my prior year, and I was catapulted to the Internet marketing stage when I won 2007 New Internet Marketing Success of the Year from the World Internet Mega Summit and was flown all-expenses paid to Singapore to speak in front of 3,400 people. After that, I developed steps as a Quantum Leap Thinker and became a successful coach, mentor, copywriter, and international platform speaker with appearances in Ireland, Dubai, Scotland, Switzerland, France, Dubai, Maldives, Canada, the United States, Kuwait, Singapore, the United Kingdom, and Australia, and have been invited to Malaysia and Jakarta (passport issue—long story), New Zealand, and many more.

What was really a blessing to me is that I had quickly become a role model for women, as in many of my speaking engagements I was the only female on stage. I make my living doing exactly what I teach—Internet marketing, motivational speaking, platform speaking, coaching, mentoring, copywriting, and my own product creation and launches—making me living proof you can make it fast. For me it was less than a year that my life had completely changed. It can be that way for you, too!

But let us take a moment to set the stage with the average outcomes, and how Quantum Leap Thinking became a big part of how it happened so fast. In most cases, I noticed many people would start by purchasing the resell rights (where you are able to sell an ebook somebody else made) or master resell rights (you are able to sell the rights to sell the ebook just like you are)—but without traffic it was useless. Join an affiliate program, but without Google AdWords or a landing page nobody found it. Even at my first attempt I created a great sales website at a cost of $5,000 through a mentor program, but because that was the only focus of the program it never got any hits. It seemed that for the "solution" or "niche" to work, the other pieces of the puzzle needed to be filled in. It is at this moment that I say "It's Not Your Fault," and with even more glee, "Everything you learned will not have been a waste, because when you walk the path and hit an area where you have experience already—you quantum leap through that section and accelerate quickly to the next." This is good news if you have been doing this and not managed to eke out your personal pot of gold. You can make money on the Internet in hours, and I hope very much that you do—but this is not the typical result (if you think about the diet philosophy it is the same). With a step-by-step approach by the end of it you will have a solid foundation to launch from. Fine-tuning it will turn it into an automated ATM machine, ringing cash in while you sleep, and giving you the complete freedom you desire. With more education on the specific area of your focus you can tweak it, add multiple streams of income, services, or simply add another completely different arm such as cash notes or real estate, and you will have a total Internet-based empire that provides you with financial freedom. It's time to become the "Maker of Your Miracles, Tracy Repchuk."

P.S. Why did I not want you to skip this step? Because this is a step-by-step book, and I want you to do *all* of the steps, *even* if you have already done it, or think you know it. You can verify that what you did is correct, or fill in a step you have not done.

Skipping steps leads to gaps, which leads to something not working. I do this for *you*.

Special Affiliate Disclosure Notice to the reader: In many cases I either give you a website name directly, or I give you a website name I own that may or may not have an affiliate connection. By all means, if you do not wish to use my affiliate connection, and want to go straight into the site after, that is just fine. The reason I create domain names for many of the links I use is for simplicity. When I originally created the book, it went straight to sites I recommended—but two things happened:

1. Some sites died before the next year's edition.

2. Better and/or cheaper options emerged. Instead of going through the whole book, or having it quickly become obsolete, I would create a master domain name I would recommend, and change it on my end with the updates.

That way the printed version remained as up-to-date as possible, at all times.

CHAPTER 1

Quantum Leap Thinking

Number One Mistake to Avoid

If there were a simple answer, would you take it? We are asked this question most of our lives this, and yet we still underestimate the power of knowing what we want. The difference between those who are really successful on the Internet and those who are struggling is the action of **goal setting**. There are people out there who have made it big by some act of nature or fluke, but in most cases when you hear about the overnight success story, there was a lot of planning to make it to that one night.

Another key difference is to think that goal setting is a passive activity. You just don't write goals down—you *expect* them to happen. You do what it takes to manifest them. There is a fundamental difference between expecting and hoping, because if you write them down and aren't wholeheartedly determined to do what it takes to make it happen, it won't.

During my Internet start-up phase in 1995 I didn't really think of it as anything more than a way to let people know about me, and serve as verification that the company exists. If I had planned for it to be more—to set a goal—today would look differently. Now I am an avid goalsetter for multiple disciplines and this was a big part of how I moved forward so fast—it has become part of my Quantum Leap Thinking approach to getting results.

During the course of my goal-setting journey in search of "The One," I did a lot of stuff backward, upside down, and in the wrong order. There are millions of pages of information out there, and tons of products, affiliate programs, and mentors. Had I seen the guidelines that we are about to go through in one place, my trip would have been even shorter. Before we can begin, you need to know where you want to go.

Begin with the End in Mind

For the past few years I have started from the end and worked my way back to how that would happen. Having goal setting as a regular part of every day, week, and year is what will make your venture a long-term success. Write down your goals and post them where you look often such as your iPhone, Android, iPad, laptop, or good old-fashioned paper stuck on your wall or fridge.

If you go rushing into the Internet like a crazy-eyed kid without a plan, you'll end up spending $5,000 before you realize that you have no idea what you bought or why. You may even be so disillusioned with the whole industry that you back off and figure it's not for you. When you begin with the end in mind you create the vision that will carry you through the hard work of getting to your goal.

When you know where you're going, it's easier to run to.

LIFE IS A BALANCING ACT

When you start a new venture you have a tendency to forget about the rest of the world and get single-minded. This isn't a good idea if you have friends and family, or want to have someone to possibly sell to in the future. When you consider all your goals it helps to make sure that you are heading toward your dreams in a way that will benefit everyone.

Life is going to involve many different things requiring your attention all at once, but if you remain aware of your goals and desires, you will continue to progress toward them.

For each element that is important to you, be sure to set a goal for it so that you always know where you are going.

Set your business goal and add items that help move you toward that. Watch for items that aren't optimizing your time and resources.

PERSONAL GOAL: (SAMPLE)

To have the financial freedom to enjoy life with my spouse and children and live the way I want.

Because work and life are so interconnected, when you make decisions in one place, it affects the other. Do activities that are relevant to your achieving your goals both personally and professionally.

MISSION STATEMENT: (SAMPLE)

To create an Internet strategy where the automation of my business, and funds created automatically allows me to donate time and money to bigger causes than myself.

A mission statement is the big-picture vision around which all your decisions revolve. This big picture prevents you from getting too caught up in the details of life, and allows you to keep some perspective as to why you are really doing something. It is easy to start for one reason, and keep going for another. When you achieve and start to experience and live your life of vision, remember to incorporate the real purpose of your life.

Have your purpose become part of a long-term strategy, and move yourself farther from the *me, me, me* box. If your market subjects detect that you are in that box, they may not be motivated to work with you, buy from you, or help you because they will question whether you will reciprocate.

BUSINESS GOAL: (SAMPLE)

To be able to get my message out in a way that is automated and doesn't require constant monitoring and that helps others reach their goals, too.

Start to work some balance into your life. Are you an accountant who could donate three hours to a senior center before tax time? Little things like that go a long way and you'll feel fantastic. It won't feel like a chore when you see how other people feel when you donate your time or knowledge. Make sure that your kids or spouse or significant other is getting some quality "you" time, too.

If you're thinking "What has this got to do with Internet marketing?" the answer is nothing and everything. Making it in this industry is a team sport. It will take time, effort, money, and a desire to help others first. If you don't emerge from your *me* box, when you have your own product ready to ship you will have an uneventful launch. Giving along the way makes the journey easier, faster, and more enjoyable. When you incorporate goals and balance into your life, you will find that when you need help, it will be there for you.

How to Get a Clean Start in Internet Marketing

Did you ever know people who run from project to project, product to product, and never finish, implement, or make a decision about what they want to do with them? This creates clutter in your mind that drowns your creativity and ability to function effectively.

Most entrepreneurs get a thousand ideas every hour—they all sound good. You can see what you could do with the latest product, but without a core focus you are confused and overwhelmed. It's called an *idea avalanche syndrome*.

Internet marketing can be one of the most overwhelming fields anyone could choose, because it is so vast and it's like getting a Harvard education every week with the content and value of information we receive every day, especially if you are a newbie.

I have found that many Internet marketing newcomers buy programs, buy products, gather information like squirrels, but forget to lay the plans in place to actually do them. Or, they lay the plan in place, but get stuck at something they can't do, or don't understand, put it back on the shelf for another day, jump on the next exciting tidbit of technology, and continue the cycle.

From this moment forward I want you to start with an organized slate. This means getting some strategies in place to help you stay on top—not under—this market.

The top two strategies I use:

1. For each Internet marketer you are following, open up an e-mail folder for that name and start to put each of the marketer's e-mails in there. This is for two reasons: one, it is easier to follow what the marketer is talking about and do any lessons you have missed; and, two, it can serve as a swipe file to get good ideas for the future.

2. Organize what you already have so that when new stuff comes in the door you will know what to do with it. You can do this in a few ways. You can have files on your hard drive for PDF files, audios, videos, ebooks, stuff you have resell rights to, and stuff you have private label rights to. This is how I'm organized, and in addition, I add a folder for each mentor program I am involved with, and everything from that program goes in there. So spend some time cleaning up and organizing what you have (you may be amazed that you can put a blog

post together tonight and start selling), and then when the new information comes in, stay on top of it.

Then approach each project in an organized fashion.

For example, if you bought an ebook with master rights and didn't ever sell any, write down the pieces you needed to be able to sell it. Break it down into steps you can do to sell it by the end of the day:

- Read the ebook if you haven't.

- Put together a website (if it came with one, this part is done). If it didn't, and you don't know how to put together a website, then go to elance.com or guru.com and post a quote request, and in a matter of hours, you will have what you need to complete this step.

- Put together a list, get a list, find people with lists. This is a big key to being able to sell an ebook, and that is having the right target audience to sell to.

- Your website is great, but you need the oxygen—people. Search for people who have products like yours, and offer to do a joint venture with them. And if you don't know what a joint venture is, find out. This is the key to understanding—if you discover that you have hit a word, acronym, or concept you don't understand that is critical to the success of your venture, take a sidetrack and get what you need to know.

- The "put together a list" step takes more steps. My first suggestion is to make sure that you have the correct autoresponder software to drive a campaign like this. Aweber is one I use and recommend. It has a reliable delivery rate, is inexpensive to start with, and easy to use.

Select one of your products, and with your recipe start to put the specifics in place for just that item. Start with the first step, and do it. If you can repeat this for each item that is still in a backlog, or half-done, then put the steps in place for those as well. Take at least one hour of your day, and devote it to getting organized, or you will have yet another year of running and surviving, without some real wealth building.

Friend Assessment

In this section I don't advocate leaving your friends and family, but you do need to examine the type of people who are in your life right now. The friends you keep determines the rate you progress in life. I was taught this by one of my mentors, Matt Bacak, who actually had to tell his mom that they couldn't speak for a while until he completed what he was working on. This was done with care and love, but if someone is being negative and causing you to doubt yourself, then you have to take care of yourself first.

Some of those negative people might be obvious—they are the ones who make you cringe when the phone rings. Remember, though, you will need people more than ever, so don't be a recluse about your journey, just stay focused, and don't let negative energy enter your space for as long as possible.

Get your most positive and encouraging friends around you, and put the others on hold.

Quantum Leap Thinking Expanded

Quantum leap thinking is another differentiator between those who climb that ladder successfully and the missing link for many others, and that is the way you think or look at things. I have been around many millionaires, and around even more "not millionaires," and I tell you, the conversations are very different.

Millionaires are actively producing and creating and enjoying life. They are excited about what you say. They are making things happen, and attracting what they need to get the job done. Hint: They did this *long before* they hit their first million.

Do you believe you can be a millionaire, or if you already are, how about a multimillionaire or a billionaire?

There are 1,011 billionaires according to *Forbes* magazine, with the youngest being 24 years old. Remember when that seemed like a number nobody would ever reach? It's like the four-minute mile—once someone proves it can be done, there are many who start to follow.

Keep moving your expectations out farther, keep running toward them, and keep excited about the journey and adventure of it, while celebrating the small steps.

Life is a game, so treat it that way in a sense of play and fun. Over the course of my journey, when things started to move quickly, I noticed a set of patterns that emerged—steps that I was taking over and over. They would have been what I heard or learned, but because they were consistent, I put them in a step-by-step format and called them *Quantum Leap Thinking*, which really is a fancy way of saying "really easy steps in life that get you farther, faster if you do them."

The following steps were inspired by people I watched, and I saw the characteristics they portrayed in order to accomplish as much as they did. By combining the successful traits of each person, the steps became powerful tools.

Twelve Practical Steps of Quantum Leap Thinking

1. **Ask yourself honestly: What are you willing to do to get your goal and ultimately your dreams?**

   Think about your goal, your dream, and then determine how much you are willing to put into making it happen. My example is that I got up at 5 A.M. many days, went to bed at 1 A.M., and got rid of habits that stole my dreams and ate my time. I had no intention of making my schedule permanent, but to get the rocket off the ground, I needed the booster power. I moved from Canada to the United States, because that is where I felt I needed to be to easily travel from show to show, and that was as an attendee—it's even more important now that I am a speaker.

2. **Listen to the whisper, then run.**

I think it was Oprah who first called a gut feeling or instinct a *whisper*. Listening to myself is something I do really well. If it sounds right, you'll know it, and then do it. Don't look back or let doubt, fear, or anything else derail your focus.

Plowing through doubt and fear creates the courage you need to do the right thing for you and your life.

3. **Say yes to opportunity or say no.**

Most people refer to this as *being decisive*. Often we are taught to say yes, but if the opportunity doesn't fit within your plans or focus, then you'll be wasting your time. So it's okay to say no, as long as you aren't saying it out of fear or lack of confidence. You won't be successful if you're drowning in indecision because you will be unable to move forward for fear of taking a wrong step or making a mistake.

4. **Always ask yourself *big* questions.**

When you're sitting at a decision point about what to do next, ask yourself *big* questions. This will cause you to shift from where you are and will attract the right answers.

An example of a big question for me was, "What do I need to do to appear as a speaker on the big stages such as the World Internet Summit?" The answer: "I need credible recognition fast by those who determine who gets to speak on those stages." The solution to doing that was to become a recognized *expert* fast. That is what writing a best seller was going to provide me. Within weeks of becoming an author, I was announced at a Matt Bacak show, I appeared the following week on Mike Litman's stage in New York City, and then three weeks later I was flown to Singapore to appear on stage with Mark Joyner, Stephen Pierce, Brett McFall, Armand Morin, Jay Abraham, Mike Filsaime, and John Childers, to name a few. Then I was a featured speaker at BritPack and the World Internet Summit Malaysia, UK, and Australia, with tons more through the year. Then during the last four months of 2010, I traveled around the world every month, appearing on my own stage.

5. **Be the general, not the army.**

I first heard this sentence from Brett McFall, and thought it was a great image. The number one way to get overwhelmed is to be everything and control everything that needs to get done. Learn to practice smart sourcing methods where you identify your strengths/weaknesses. Spend 80 percent of your time on your strengths and outsource the rest.

Go to www.easyoutsourcingnow.com or www.getafreelancer.com or www.elance.com to farm everything else out. Outsource to them while you work on the important stuff. Yanik Silver had the same advice when I interviewed him; in fact, he said he considered himself a technophobe.

Even though farming out might cost you a couple of hundred dollars to get something done, lost time will cost you far more. Time is money even if you're not making any yet. You need to accelerate your pace to keep you motivated, and nothing kills motivation more than trudging through crappy jobs you hate.

If you want something simple done, like putting up a wordpress blog, or doing an article, you can spend $5 and get great service at www.Fiverr.com.

6. **Plan for a quantum leap.**

   When you want something, planning is a critical step. Most results don't happen by fluke—you need to put a plan in place to start to make things happen faster.

   I plan a "big advancement/quantum leap strategy" item every three months. This means that I put in 120 percent for this item in order to complete the strategy in a faster time frame.

7. **Understand your metrics.**

   Internet marketing works on statistics. Learn them, and understand how they affect what you do. If your statistics show that no one is opening your e-mail, fix your subject line. If no is one clicking to your offer, fix your e-mail. If no one is buying at your sales page, fix it, and if you aren't getting subscribers, fix your landing page. Metrics let you know where the problem is you need to fix. Track statistics for your e-mail sent, opened, click rates, opt-ins to your landing page, and conversions to sales.

8. **Invest in yourself—get a mentor.**

   Invest in mentors, educational materials, training— these are critical to advancing the skills you have and ensure that you get a good grasp of the tasks you are outsourcing.

I went from total obscurity—nobody knew me in this industry—to best-selling author and Internet marketing success story. It took a lot of investing in myself, training, studying, reading, and getting coaching. Then I advanced to award-winning coach, mentor, and internationally renowned speaker. Step-by-step I invested in mentors, and to this day I still do.

9. **Become a *freedom agent*.**

I first heard this term from Mark Joyner. Mark is known as the "Godfather of Internet Marketing" and, like Timothy Ferriss of *The 4-Hour Work Week*, talks about creating your life by shaping your actions around the end result you are seeking. In the beginning this is your mission statement, but now you want to add the how, and constantly be crafting your strategies toward making more money in less time.

10. **Dare to be different.**

In the world of Internet marketing you need to follow the formulas to easily achieve desired results, but when it comes to product design, writing your story, using your unique proposition, and attaching your flair—that is what will get you noticed. This is where you shine. In our industry, some of the dare-to-be-different pioneers to watch are Dan Kennedy and Jay Abraham.

11. **Make your goal a "no matter what" moment.**

Have you really said to yourself that you are going to make that happen, and tag that with no matter what? What commitment have you given your goal, and where does your goal sit as a priority in your life? That is what I asked. It was a big step because I was comfortable, I could have done what I did for years and survived. At 42, even though I was young, this was like starting again, and I became determined to be successful fast. So for a while that meant no vacations, long hours, and making all sorts of changes in my habits, to make "no matter what" moments.

12. **Massive action.**

Action is good, but if you want faster results, you're going to give more than you are used to over a period of time. For the goal you set as a quantum leap goal, this is where 120 percent needs to be focused at increased intervals. Action—massive action—is a way to take control of the moment you are in, the direction you are going, and the results you want to achieve.

CELEBRATE SMALL VICTORIES

What happens when you have a big goal is that you forget to celebrate the little steps along the way and when you do that, it feels like a very long road.

Be sure to keep in mind that making money can be easy. If it has become hard, you probably have considerations (things you were told) that you started to believe and eventually they became reality and complicated the process for you.

Follow your goal, and in addition, have a chart where you celebrate the smaller steps along the way.

For example, for Internet marketing celebrate:

- First 10 subscribers in your database.
- Your first $1 on automatic.

- $100—Go for lunch.

- $1,000—Go for dinner.

- $10,000—Buy a treat or go on a vacation.

- $100,000—Pay down or buy a house.

- $1,000,000—Treat of your choice.

- Continue . . . .

Always Celebrate the Victories, Even When You Have Made It Big

In addition to celebrating the small steps as you move closer to your ultimate goals and dreams, remember when you hit a milestone along the way that you acknowledge this and celebrate in a way that really reminds you how far you've come. Maybe you finally published that book, or had a five-figure day, or reached that original goal you set of six figures in your business. Celebrate that accomplishment, and then set your next big goal. Then always remember to keep doing that so that you experience the joy of those moments before you keep moving forward.

With statistics like these, you can be next: 1,011 billionaires according to *Forbes*; more than 10 million millionaires—and it grows by an average of 500,000 per year and by 1,400 people per day. Do you believe you can be one of them? Good! Then we are getting closer.

FAST CASH

The question I always get asked is how can I make some fast cash. I have read many ways, but only a few produced results for me. There is no magic pill in this industry, and when you hear miraculous results, understand that there is a backstory that created that moment.

Here are my tips that may work for you in getting fast cash:

- **Leverage.** The fastest way I made money was when I took a skill/service I already had and made a sales page around it. I also posted it in my blog. Within two days of doing this I had made $5,497—someone purchased my skills as a copywriter and web designer and that was the fee I charged to create a landing page.

- **Sell your stuff.** The next way I made fast cash was with Craigslist (www.Craigslist.com).

  My daughter took stuff we had in our garage that was driving me crazy and sold it for the price I was asking. My kids do this all the time and now when they want new stuff, they sell the old. In fact, my daughter Celeste has taken this to an art form, and can make up to $300 per week doing this.

- **Sell on auction.** My daughter also makes cash by selling her stuff on eBay (www.ebay.com). The difference between Craigslist and eBay is that Craigslist is local and the buyers pick up. You usually have to ship with eBay.

- **Offer your services or stuff cheap.** My kids offer services, drawings, YouTube account setup, all sorts of stuff to make $5 on www.Fiverr.com.

- **Become a freelancer.** For any of the outsourcing services (for example, www.elance.com) you can be a service provider if you have a skill you can offer up there.

- **Hold a teleseminar.** A fun way I earned money was with my first teleseminar. (A teleseminar is when you go on the phone on a conference line that others dial into and listen. I go into much detail later on how to do one.) It was someone else's product. I offered to put the whole teleseminar together, just to get familiar with the process (as I had attended enough teleseminars to see how you did them, now I wanted to actually run one).

  I invited my Twitter followers to a free teleseminar (I wasn't even on Facebook yet at that time).

There the owner of the product educated on the steps of his topic, then sold his coaching package. I made $497 per sale—it was magic. After I built my own list, I got teleseminar training from Alex Mandossian and now I hold webinars to sell when I want to buy something in cash. (These are similar in concept to a teleseminar only instead of the attendee just being able to listen, they attend online and can watch it like a show. I do webinars because my topic is complex and pictures and diagrams help to simplify it. Teleseminars are great for interview type concepts.)

So approach someone with a product, see if you can do it all for that person, and get a cut. Hit someone new, not a guru, as newbies have high expectations for attendees. I had 13 attendees on my own first teleseminar and seven bought. You can get started for free (www. FreeConferenceCalling.com).

- **Sell Clickbank products properly.** This brings us directly to www.Clickbank.com. Many people are told when they get started to just go to Clickbank, grab a product, and start selling. If you sell to social media followers directly, you will risk getting your account shut because in the Terms of Service (TOS) of most social media platforms it states you aren't allowed to sell. You will see in many cases people are selling and getting away with it, so more follow suit. However, just because it's being done, you don't want to end up being that person who gets singled out and end up with your account closed. It's like speeding down a highway and you get pulled over by the police and you say, "Everyone else was speeding too," this isn't going to get you out of your ticket.

Looking from another angle as well is "Do you like getting sold on social media?" *Yes!* If you don't like being sold in an environment that is supposed to be about engaging and enlightening, think how your followers feel. For some people this is a complete business model (although I would *never* recommend this), because selling through social media is a form of spam, and if any provider gets a report about you, *all* of your followers and your accounts are deleted. Bye, bye business model, and I have seen this happen. So don't do something you don't like having done to you. Selling on social media makes for a bad start. It's one thing to invite people to a webinar, it's another to sell them directly.

I recommend selling Clickbank products by picking one you like, checking it out for real, writing a review on your blog about it, writing articles about it and submitting those, putting a permanent link on your blog, and creating a YouTube video about it. If you can, find a membership site product versus ebook for monthly recurring income potential. You will need to switch up keywords and do multiple articles and postings, but it can lead to some activity and sales.

I made about $50 to $450 a month in my early start on Clickbank. It was *not* my focus; anything I sold there was usually a specific promotion of something I bought and liked, so I would release an e-mail about it in my autoresponder system, and when people hit it, it would generate sales. Once you have a big list, this can be a lucrative field—again, though, your goal is your own product that is a business. *Before* you do any of this though, make sure you get a landing page in place, send *all* traffic to that, then send them to the Clickbank offer. That way you build your list, and you can even create an autoresponder series to take the time to sell visitors if they do not buy right away. You will have one landing page and an autoresponder series per product.

- **Sell your report.** The hardest money to make on the Internet is your first dollar. If you want, when you create your landing page, make the report or freebie gift a good one, and sell it for $1 versus free for name and e-mail.

  Once you break the seal, you will have some faith in the process, and a hunger to make more. You can then change it back to free, or keep this one and create another landing page for list-building volume.

None of these is pure Internet marketing, but it is hard to make money when you don't know what you're doing yet. The key sometimes is to get some cash so you can get a mentor. I spent every cent I made in the beginning on mentors for the steps I needed. If you have no list, who do you sell to?

There are probably many more fast cash tips out there—some are real, some are not when you are starting from scratch. The key is to focus on what is real—and that is to select something you are passionate about, build a landing page, product, sales page, and start selling.

Create a Freedom Lifestyle

Chapter 1 Action Plan

- Set 3 goals.
- Get organized on your computer. Create files and e-mail folders.
- Create your victory chart.
- Select a fast cash method and give it a try.

CHAPTER 2

Preparing for Power

DAY 1—MAKE YOUR MARKET COUNT

One of the most important steps I take with my clients is to find out first what they are passionate about. Why sell an ebook just because it makes money when you have no connection to that field at all? The list you build and the effort get you nowhere when it comes to your goals (remember those from Chapter 1 and your long-term mission). Here are the criteria I go over with my clients.

Top Six Factors When Picking a Niche

1. You need to pick something that motivates you to keep on going if the going gets tough.

2. Do you have knowledge about it, or would you have to pay for someone else to get the data or write the product for you? (I recommend that you pick something you know about.)

3. Is there a built-in audience that you can easily target?

4. Does this target market have money—in other words, the ability to buy what you are offering?

5. Is there a problem you can solve, a pain you can eliminate, or an obsessive market you can serve?

6. Do you have a story you can integrate into the product, or know of someone you can talk about to personalize the experience?

In general, choose something you can make money from, streamline and automate, and continue or recur. Can others make money for you (affiliate) or can you sell something once and have it continue to automatically generate month after month?

If your product doesn't satisfy those criteria, then this is a warning that your niche may not turn out to be the cash machine you thought and might be best kept as a hobby. Remember, you are trying to make money at whatever your online endeavor is, so keep looking. Your focus is to select the market/area you want to be involved in. We get more specific in the product chapter later, but at this point we just want to start to wrap your strategy around a concept that fits the above criteria.

While putting together your goals and steps, you probably discovered a niche—an area that really interests you such as horses, fitness, diet—or if you are sticking to Internet marketing, it could be fields such as Google AdSense, eBay, or affiliate programs. Keep the ultimate goal in mind, which is to create your own product.

The top seven markets as of this writing are real estate; online trading; Forex and wealth building; Internet, fitness, health, and beauty; identity theft; credit restoration; and early retirement and life extension.

If you want to find out what is currently trending, go to www.google.com/trends/hottrends.

The problem with trends is that they may not have staying power. That is why the above seven are great starters, but also remember that because of the competition in those fields you have to drill down precisely to your niche.

If nothing has sprung to mind yet, use these 16 questions to help get you thinking:

1. What do you like to do?

2. What skills do you have?

3. How would your friends describe you?

4. What books do you enjoy reading?

5. What types of hobbies do you have?

6. What computer skills do you have?

7. What knowledge do you have?

8. Where have you traveled?

9. What problems can you solve with your knowledge?

10. What type of advice do you give out when asked?

11. What magazines do you read?

12. Do you have a bad habit you'd like to kick?

13. Are you married? Single? Got kids?

14. What have been your greatest successes?

15. What training or education have you had?

16. Do you like public speaking? Talking on the phone?

You could literally ask yourself hundreds of questions, but I chose these as the top ones to help you fine-tune what you would like to devote your time to. Realize that you know many things and have skills and knowledge that are unique to you. Figure out your message, and *decide* on a niche.

Here are some places you can research about niche markets. You can take advantage of focus groups and social networking sites as well. This section lets you see if what you have chosen is a viable money maker based on the searches or popularity of it.

Search Inspirations

- www.google.com/trends/hottrends

- www.GoogleEasySearch.com

- https://groups.google.com/forum/?fromgroups#!browse

- www.google.com

- www.Groups.yahoo.com and www.yahoo.com
- www.linkedin.com/directory/groups/
- Check out the top picks on Amazon or eBay

You can also use research tools such as:

- www.Alexa.com
- www.copernic.com

Once your niche is selected, then get all the knowledge you can about that area or skill, or join the appropriate affiliate program, so you can start your 31-day plan.

Four things to strive for:

1. Become the best at your niche, and continuously strive to achieve that. Watch what the current person in that position does, and do it, too. If you can, carve out your own niche pocket and create your own category.

2. While you are building yourself to be number one, act like you already are. Look for ways to be in front of your niche audience or target market constantly.

3. Position yourself as a leading authority. Provide information on that topic or skill and then start to think about what you're going to produce or sell that fits that niche. Make sure your goals and your niche align.

4. Think old school when you set up your website—brand, logo, and unique selling proposition that make you easy to recognize, match what your target market expects, and in one simple sentence let them know what you can do for them.

Websites You Must Have

If you already have active websites when you get started with your new venture, I can show you how they will work within your branding identity. The key to this section is how you arrange it all to maximize your profit potential.

Traditionally, companies would go one of two routes:

1. A corporate/brochure-type site that talks about who, what, where, when, and why, and anything in between. Some sites are even bold enough to ask for the visitor's e-mail address.

2. A site similar to the above, only it's really fancy, bold, colorful, flashy, and . . . not working.

If the traffic hits are abysmal and your site is not selling for you, then why spend the money?

Four Types of Websites/Pages You Must Have and Why

1. **Branding.** This site contains all products and services. This is where most companies spend their budget. This is where you send contacts you meet to give them a broad overview of your company or you. An example of this is my branding site www.TracyRepchuk.com.

2. **Sales letter.** This is one page and it's often a long site that highlights the benefits of one product or service.

   Not many companies have this type of site. This is how you get the sale. It can be really effective when used in conjunction with an e-mail-based marketing campaign, and/or it is the go-to page after a landing page/ squeeze page. It can be copywriting or video—either way, this page requires time and effort, but is worth it. An example of this is www.InternetSuccessMastery.com/.

3. **Blog.** This is a journal-type site that keeps everyone up-to-date with what you are doing, and/or developments with your products or services.

    You post your articles here and keep in touch with your prospects and customers. This is how you rapidly communicate with your prospects and get a fast Google presence for free. An example is www .IMTracyRepchuk.com, which is a redirect domain for www.TracyRepchuk.com/blog.

4. **Landing page/squeeze page.** This is the most important page your company will ever have, and only 7 percent of the Internet population has it.

    These are the companies that are making millions, and doing very little work for it. This is how you capture your visitor so that you can build a relationship with your prospect and upsell to an unlimited degree. An example of this is www.MarketingSolutionsForBusiness.com.

Flow Overview

Advanced strategies you can add:

- An upsell or one-time offer is a web page that appears once visitors have purchased. The page encourages them to buy additional add-on items or a completely new offer.

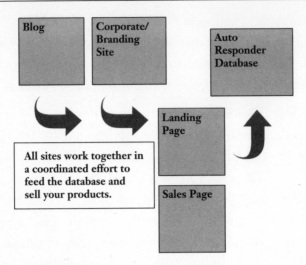

Figure 2.1   Visitor Flow

- Downsell is when visitors haven't purchased from your sales page. A pop-up appears and asks them to purchase a lower-priced option.

- Tell-a-friend strategy is a form that requests visitors tell friends about you in exchange for a free bonus gift.

Day 2—Powerful Branding Strategies

In the beginning your company probably had one master website as the tool to educate others about who you are and what you do. That is the branding/corporate site. In many cases, though, this was represented as all that you needed. If you are going to have a site on the Internet wouldn't you rather it made money, converted customers to clients, and got you attention from Google or other sites, too?

If your website isn't generating one of two things—money or convertible leads—then you need to start to put together your branding strategy starting with:

1. A landing page

2. A blog

3. A sales page

4. Branding—all the information, integrating sites (1–3)

If you're having a heart attack about now, visions of thousands of dollars down the toilet and months of hard work and effort, not to worry, because you need that site, too! This is a great site for the purpose it was built for—telling others about you, letting them know you're good, reputable, and the site is a central place to see all of your products and services. What this site is not good for, though, is conversion of visitors to purchasers.

Do you know what the conversion rate for leads or sales for this type of site is? Less than 1 percent. If you get 10,000 visitors, then 100 of those might become a lead, and without a sales page less than 1 percent convert to a sale. That is one out of 10,000 who will possibly buy. Unless your product is $1,000,000, and you only need to sell one per year, then this is a model that won't work for you.

A landing page to a sales page with blog support and a corporate or personal presence is the combination that will establish your brand identity and sales-pulling power. Then you can add social media and really get some action.

Domain Names Make a Difference

Selecting the correct domain names is critical. It is a key strategy to establishing your brand identity and search ability. The domain name you may already have is probably used for your "Branding Site." Now we need to get domain names for your landing page, blog, and sales page.

If you already have a pile of domain names waiting to be useful, then use one if applicable. What you want to remember here, though, is that your branding identity will be with you for a while. So for your master site if you are the brand or blog, I would recommend you use your name; for example, www .TracyRepchuk.com (if your name is not available, get something close, for example, www.AskTracyRepchuk.com). I also have www.TracyRepchuk.mobi for a mobile site (I talk about this in a future chapter), www.TracyRepchukLive.com, and www .IMTracyRepchuk.com.

So get what you need to secure your identity/brand.

Your landing page/squeeze page, which is your niche/ product feeder page, needs to be keyword-based. Match the exact phrase of what people would search for, and buy the domain name for it (for example, the Google keyword phrase www .NewBusinessMarketingStrategies.com), and for your sales page this will be your product name. This page does not have to be keyword-based. Memorable is more important. My quantum leap product is www.QuantumLeapSecrets.com. In addition, because this is a whole product line I will be creating, I also bought www.QuantumLeapGoals.com, QuantumLeapThinking .com, www.QuantumLeapConnection.com, www.QuantumLeap Launch.com, and many others to complete the brand.

TIP

Domain names can be purchased from so many different places. I use godaddy.com, with prices at about $9.95. You can buy the site for 1 to 10 years. I buy it for two years, as this helps with search rankings, but doesn't break the bank. Also search on Google.com with "Godaddy Coupon code" and it will discount the name to about $7.47. You will see the prompt at checkout. If you feel like going through my affiliate link, go to www.InternetMarketingISP.com.

If you don't have a hosting provider, these guys are good for that, too. Great support.

Don't be afraid to buy sites that fit your strategy, because once Internet real estate is gone, the game of "I wish I had bought that when I had a chance" is a costly one. For the cost, it is worth buying and holding onto domain names until you are ready. This isn't an area to be conservative.

Draw a sketch on paper that shows how you would like the flow to go from blog, to landing page, to sales page, from corporate/branding site, and have the domain names (like the diagram from earlier about flow overview) labeled. This will also help you later when you are tying the project together in your autoresponder and payment system.

Blogging Your Way to Becoming a Brand

A blog (web log) is a web journal/log where you can quickly talk to your audience without any need for web knowledge. It is as simple as going to blogger.com or wordpress.com and setting up an account for free.

The better strategy, though, is to place your blog underneath your master domain name, which is more difficult but in the long run will get you the Google search benefits you crave. This will become the place you put your quick updates, your articles, your product announcements, and your product links. It's a bit like a branding site only far easier to use. The blog formats instantly and lets you create a dialogue with your target market through comments.

Most importantly, though, this is your fastest way to get ranked for keywords and your name with Google and other search engines, plus you can distribute your posts quickly and easily through mass distribution sites for blogs such as www.pingomatic.com and www.pingler.com.

There are hundreds of blog services and some reside within specific niche areas, which may be better suited to your product. Simply go to Yahoo! or Google, and type "your niche" blogs and you'll have plenty of options to choose from.

When branding your identity, blogs can be a big part of the success for a full-scope campaign. As you may know when you are putting together a campaign for a product launch or company launch, there are a number of pieces for which you should start to lay the foundation. These originate from the four types of websites and their purpose.

Most companies start off with their personal or corporate site. With that all ready to go, visitors can check out their address and product details. When you are launching or building the product around a specific identity/person, personalize it because a blog is the perfect place to do this.

You want to make your blog the central depository for all your articles, general announcements, and for telling visitors what you are up to so you can help or advise them. The best thing is that you don't need to be technical. You can quickly post ideas, interact with people, share photos, and more!

Talk to your audience at every opportunity. Tell them what cool things you have discovered. In essence, it is your way to get personal. These people are possibly your future purchasers, so by letting them know who you are, and that you care and are here, they feel connected to you.

17 Tips to Make Your Blog a Screaming Success

1. Avoid blog services that do not allow you to use your own domain name. Make sure you purchase your name as a dot-com (i.e., www.IMTracyRepchuk.com) and redirect it to your blog. That helps with the branding. You can also repeat this for a tagline, too, if you want, such as my "Marketing Makeover Maestro."

2. Make your template stand out by customizing it with your picture, affiliate programs, websites you like, whatever is appropriate for the market and you. Simply select tools from the menu bar and upload your images.

3. Research and use keywords in your blog post title, in the body of the post, and use anchor text when you link to previous posts you've made, and in your title.

4. Optimize your blog and take advantage of RSS options, social bookmark links, title tags, meta tags, meta descriptions, and meta keywords.

5. Find authoritative blogs, websites, and portals and outbound links to them.

6. Format your archived posts, related posts, and add Google AdSense and affiliate program links and make some money.

7. Make sure you are tracking statistics and monitoring inbound traffic links. (You can use Google Analytics to do this.)

8. Take advantage of special features such as podcasts and video abilities.

9. Post regularly. If you post articles you have written, you aren't necessarily creating new content every day but organizing where it goes. For a personal brand identity blog, daily is always good. If you are trying to become an authoritative blog, anywhere from a few times a week to daily is recommended.

10. Submit your blog URL (universal resource locator; i.e., domain name) to search engines.

11. Create and distribute a press release announcing your blog. Continue to do this for major announcements that you post there as well. Public relations (PR) is an ongoing animal, and is critical to the success of any campaign.

12. Join relevant social groups, forums, and discussion threads and post comments that are helpful on appropriate blogs.

13. Make a point of finding other industry-related blogs or authoritative sites and participate on these, too.

14. If you find a blog link in your statistics, visit and post a reply thanking him or her.

15. Build a relationship with other bloggers, especially those who link to you.

16. Mention popular bloggers by name in your blog; the traffic will help you and serve as a keyword.

17. If you want to make money with your blog add Google AdSense, Clickbank, Amazon, or eBay to the template and archives and affiliate product links, and you've got double the pleasure for your buck.

A blog is an easy way to get started quickly for free, plus a great way to get a really good ranking in the search engines versus the normal grind up the ladder when starting a new site. Last tip: Frequently go to www.pingomatic.com and let Google and others know that you've updated your site.

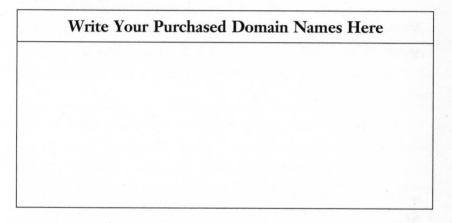

Write Your Purchased Domain Names Here

Add Your Date as Well to Help with Renewals

> **TIP**
>
> When buying your domain names, don't buy privacy or let them add it free for the first year. It will cost you twice as much for every domain name, and there is no need to hide. And chances are you will forget at renewal and be charged.

DAY 3—SQUEEZE OUT A LANDING PAGE

After spending almost 23 years in the computer industry I frequently get asked by clients, "Why isn't my site giving me what I need?" When I ask what they are looking for, they say, "Leads, sales, and traffic." I ask, "Well, do you have a landing page, sales page, and autoresponder system?"

This is about the point that they either get quiet on the phone, or their eyes glaze over. They tell me they have a website with all of their products. I tell them it's a great start, but it is just one piece of the puzzle. You have to add a whole new approach if you expect sales and leads.

A landing page is the reason you can make money while you sleep. It's a specialized page that visitors are directed to in order to capture the visitor's name and e-mail address. It is done to target market them on a particular product or send directly to a sales page. The landing page has become increasingly more important in the vastness of the Internet to start to create a relationship with your visitors. It allows you to connect with them automatically via an e-mail message that is personalized and gets sent to them at a set interval. It is like personally e-mailing or calling them to educate them on your product or service, without taking you any time.

It is also good to reinforce the message of a sales page because, with the time constraints of most people, you only have about eight seconds to get their attention, so you bite-size the information to them by using an automated system called an *autoresponder* to take advantage of the attention span of the average consumer.

The landing page is a vital step in the overall strategy of successful Internet marketing, and although some may tell you it is a dead form, those who don't like landing pages are usually the ones who have not had success with them. This goes back to my point with this technology and that is to use experienced creators of them, and "follow the cash" (which, if you recall, means to listen to the person with more money than you).

There are people who have paid $20,000 for an effective landing page campaign—and it has more than paid off for them. That is how important this page is. Landing pages often promote you along with a free or low-cost offer, perhaps a membership to something, which creates a list of people who know you, like you, trust you, and buy from you.

In a time where communication is slipping and more people are getting spammed, getting permission to send e-mail is mandatory.

The bottom line with landing pages is that they work for exactly what you want them to. They serve as the doorway to your organization and capture the visitors' contact information by asking, not by taking. Visitors opt-in, willfully, wanting to find out more.

Start to think about what difference a page like this could mean to your company, and most importantly, start your campaign and marketing efforts by getting one. This type of page combines Internet marketing tools such as autoresponders that allow you to turn your computer from a quiet site on the World Wide Web to a mass-marketing machine where you can build relationships, generate leads, and create a profitable blueprint for the next stage of your business.

If someone doesn't think you need a landing page, then they're either the competition, or don't want you to grow. So watch what is happening in the industry, and follow the Internet marketers who have turned this into an art form.

Landing Page Secrets Revealed

Landing/squeeze pages have a formula. There is technology behind how the eyes move on the screen, scrolling reactions, keeping the opt-in above the fold, colors, fonts, size, pictures, video, audio, location of everything, keywords, and most important—the copywriting. Headlines, subheadlines, opt-in requests, testimonials—this is an art form. People pay dearly for precise direct sales copy, with the average well-written site starting at about $5,400.

A good landing page can't be bought from a box, created from a template (it can be started), or copied in its entirety. Even the selection of a landing page domain name is critical to the success of the page. This isn't something that software can usually tell you. You don't need to be a copywriting guru, but you need to learn what the headline should say. Hire someone to write this for you. Try elance.com or getafreelancer.com. The cost is about $50 if you have something for the writer to model. For the rest, though, you can have stuff written for you, but it has to have your story integrated or there will be no connection to you from the audience (more on this later).

Copywriting is the art that produces leads and sales. It isn't HTML programming or design that makes this technology unique, it's the writing. Get trained if you want to be in control of this aspect—and copywriting is a skill I encourage you to invest in. One effective headline can pay for all your copywriting training in one launch.

If you are not well known yet, your squeeze page should be short. The eyes will start in the upper left, move to the right, come down the right, and move back over to the left. Be aware of loud pictures or distractions that prevent visitors from opting-in and keep that above the fold line (the screen).

Prehead—Target prime prospect

Headline—Red or maroon

"Remember to Cap the First Letter"

Deck—Arouses curiosity, reinforces headline

Your picture, video greeting, or testimonial	Opt-in offer
Your address and phone number	Opt-in box
	Security/privacy policy
	Anti-spam message

Landing pages are a precise formula, and although you need to test it for your industry, your target market, and play with varying headline formats there are six factors for ultimate success:

1. The headline is usually in red or maroon, contains caps at the first letter of each word, and contains quotes.

2. Preferred fonts are Georgia, Tahoma, and Times New Roman, Italics, size 60.7.

3. For testimonials, keep them short with the full name and city of the provider. Use longer versions on the sales page.

4. If you see a layout you love, borrow the layout. If you have MS-Expression, you simply select a site you like, go to **File, Edit within MS-Expression,** and it loads. Get rid of all of the content within the layout you like, and add your own. This is a fast and simple way to get started. For other editors use the **import** function.

5. Make the page background gray, white, or light or navy blue. Watch the industry standards from other popular pages, though, because this changes frequently.

6. Add a tracking tag to be sure you are monitoring your stats. This comes from your autoresponder. Have only one link. Visitors either leave or opt-in.

Bottom line—*one purpose*—get visitors to opt-in. Go to www.MarketingSolutionsForBusiness.com for a sample.

Top 10 Ways to Improve Your Landing Page

Many people don't think of this, but landing pages are an art form so I recommend that you don't leave this in the hands of your buddy or you'll still be wondering what the big deal is about them, while the rest of us convert leads to sales.

If you spend money on only one marketing action this year, I recommend that it be a landing/squeeze page. If you really want to take a stab at it yourself, here are 10 tips that will help you navigate this new territory.

1. **Follow the layout that works.**

   Have you ever noticed that when something works people just can't help but wonder whether if they did "x," it would be better? That's great if you know what you are doing, but when something works, be careful what you mess with. If it doesn't call for fancy don't get fancy. Find the template that works for your industry, and duplicate it.

2. **Research.**

   Take a look at your industry and then Google search to find landing page sites in it. Then use Alexa.com to check out the page ranking. The combination of this allows you to see what works for your industry content-wise. Keep the profile of your visitors in mind when adding content and target them specifically. Remember to add key search terms while you're at it.

3. **Don't add what isn't needed.**

   The purpose of the landing page is to do one thing—get the e-mail address and name of the visitors so that you can build relationships with them. Distractions can destroy your conversions. Don't add any other links, and give them a clear message as to what you are offering and why they should subscribe. The only way out should be to leave or subscribe.

4. **Personalize.**

   Two ways you can dramatically increase your opt-in ratio is to add your picture in the left-hand column below the headline area and if it is possible, add your signature at the bottom. Let visitors know that you are a real person and this is a real offer. Get rid of anything that isn't essential to the conversion process. Even better, make it a video.

5. **Solve a problem or promote the benefits.**

   A great way to get good conversion is to use your text wisely. Make sure you let visitors know how you can solve a problem, or how the amazing benefits they are about to receive can change their lives. You need to give them a huge reason to opt-in.

6. **Follow the page eye-line strategy.**

   The eye follows a specific pattern, so make sure the content you need visitors to see matches. In addition, you want all critical information to be above the screen line or virtual fold (the bottom of the screen before scrolling). Watch out for the number of pictures you have that may distract and pull from your opt-ins, and keep this to a minimum. You want their eyes to go to the opt-in box. This is not a place for ads, sidebars, navigation bars, or much of anything except getting their e-mail and name.

7. **Display your anti-spam message.**

   Make sure you make visitors immediately aware that you will not use their list for any other purpose than what they are opting in for. You won't rent, sell, or do anything that would compromise your relationship with the people who now gave you their trust.

8. **Opt-in basics.**

   Optimize your opt-in by making sure you don't ask for too much information. If you are using auto-responders as your campaign to keep in touch, just get an e-mail and first name. If you have a high-end product that may require some personal communication, then also ask for a phone number. In general, less is easier to get, and you can ask for more later.

9. **Make it urgent.**

You want visitors to think that if they don't opt-in and take your offer then they are missing out on some important information. You must make the need for them to opt-in urgent. Limited time offer. Today only. Make your opt-in bonus appear time-sensitive. Not only will this increase your conversion rate but it will also add to the relationship building, as you give them something for free.

10. **Test and tweak.**

Always watch the statistics of your landing page with respect to the number of visitors and the number who opted-in. If this isn't an acceptable rate for your industry, change something and repost. Then watch again. Constantly analyze the results (this is done in your domain name back panel where you registered or you can add Google Analytics if you are familiar with that). Modify until you get a rate that really helps your business grow and gives you someone to talk to and build a relationship with.

Here are some details to review:

- Is the whole page focused on one objective?

- Is there an urgent need or incentive to opt-in?

- Do you have all of the critical elements?

- Is critical information above the fold?

- Is there any information that you do not need and is distracting?

- Does the page add to your overall strategy and brand?

- Is the whole page cohesive?

Last thoughts: One more great debate that revolves around this page is whether you should have audio and video on your pages. I go into more detail later, but my preference is to have a video. It increases the experience, but the bigger question is really: Should it come on right away or be turned on by the visitor? That question is answered in Chapter 4.

With a landing page in place your business can be on an entirely new level of automated money generation with visitors who become part of your permission-based marketing system.

This isn't a luxury item, it is a necessity.

Tip

Skyrocket Your Profits

Here it is—your ultimate, money-making, viral marketing website scenario: Have a squeeze/landing page lead to a sales page, to a one-time offer, to a tell-a-friend page (offer a free gift for leads), and close with a $1 trial offer to your continuity/membership club.

Write down your product strategy and what you would offer at each stage. If you can, begin with the end in mind. Know what your back end is and work your way to the landing page. It helps you with the flow and structure.

Landing Page	Sales Page	One Time Offer or Tell-a-Friend* Prompt	Downsell (on Exit)
Collects visitor information	Long sales website that sells them on your product or service	Do a one-time offer, then offer a free gift if they can refer three to five friends, and easily create your own marketing campaign	$1 membership trial offer for 21 days, then regular price

*Viral friend generator

TIP

WANT TO MAKE YOUR FIRST $1 ON THE INTERNET?

Get a good ebook or create an informative report and charge $1 to opt-in. This will limit your opt-ins, but a first sale is a barrier for some people and if you get it over fast, perhaps you will see how Internet marketing works. Then you can change to the free method later, or test with two different landing pages.

Websites That Work for You

The sales page is a critical factor in the success of your Internet marketing campaign and is the page that follows the landing page or tell-a-friend page. My first try at a sales page was in the Corey Rudl days when I hired a mentor. At the time it got only slightly better results than the "branding" site, not the windfall I was expecting. At that time I was missing the critical landing page in front of it, and a traffic strategy.

What did the landing/squeeze page get me afterward? The capture of the visitor's e-mail and name so that I had a chance to build a relationship if the person didn't immediately buy. This opened up permission-based contacts; they'll know who you are and that you want to help them. In a world full of "not so nice people and scammers," this gives you a chance to build trust long enough to show them what they need. If you have a product that is needed and wanted, you want and need to get it out there. And if you treat visitors well, you'll build a list of people who know you, like you, trust you, and buy from you.

Hopefully you can start to see that no capture and no sales page results in a flat site. You need the number of contacts to be high so that your conversion rate can increase and your profits, sales, and lifestyle can flourish. These are important visitors because they came to you. You didn't cold-call them or blast to a purchased e-mail list in hopes of some sort of response (which, by the way, you will get, and it won't be pretty). These are people who expressed an interest in your message (from your landing page) and possibly want what you have.

The purpose of a landing page is to get you contacts. Contacts = Prospects for Sales. The purpose of a sales page is to sell and close the deal. In between those two sites, you build a relationship.

Some Technical Tips

- If you need to transfer large files between yourself and perhaps a contracted worker or friends, e-mail is not a good tool. Use www.TransferBigFiles.com.

- When you need to upload your software to your ISP, you often need software to do this called *FTP* (file transfer protocol software). You can get a free tool called *Filezilla* (www.filezilla-project.org) that will upload your web pages.

- If you don't have a web editor to create web pages you can use WordPress and templates, or get a free editor at www.WebEditorForFree.com.

DAY 4—OPT-IN INSIGHTS

An opt-in is a box that appears on a landing page website that requests you provide your information (such as name and e-mail address) in return for a gift. You have probably encountered many opt-ins on various websites, and the offers range from membership, tips, a free ebook, newsletter, report, video, or audio, but whatever the offer is, the key is to make sure it complements what you plan on doing. It is meant to highlight the product you ultimately want them to buy.

For example, if you have a beauty site, a great opt-in offer would be a beauty tips ebook, report, newsletter, or a chance to win a free beauty gift. I change my offer often. I rotate among a chapter peek, free ebook, report, video intro, membership, or audio interview. I have signed up for my share of opt-ins containing any of the above offers and more. The more you give, the better your opt-in ratio.

When considering your Internet marketing strategy, the thing to remember is that once you have visitors as subscribers you have to act fast to keep them connected. The whole reason for an opt-in is to build your list and a relationship with them. These are possible sales for you but most people are also savvy, and if you don't keep them interested or educated, or provide them with offers that help, they'll opt-out mighty fast.

The offer though is just the start. Your success really comes from your autoresponders and your sales page. You need to welcome them immediately, have another piece of information go out in the next run, and then use the formula to send the rest. When you get more familiar with the process, you want to add split-testing to see which offer produces the best conversion ratio (this is the percentage of visitors to people who actually opt-in). To do this you can rotate the landing page index, have three different campaigns running from different web domains that merge into the same list, or use a product that rotates just the headline or other specific fields. Test and tweak as often as you can to improve your statistics, because this is the gateway to your sales.

Write here some product freebie gift ideas:

_____

_____

_____

_____

_____

DAY 5—SELECT AN AUTORESPONDER

This is a critical step in your entire business logic and foundation. You can choose whatever works for you and there are many autoresponders out there, but I can tell you that after trying many of them and learning new software, then scrapping it, and constantly moving my database around and repeating this cycle, and having failed e-mail campaigns, and being accused of being a spammer to my own database, I finally figured out the magic combination.

First off, before you do anything, if you have your domain name and ISP already and plan on hosting your own auto-responder, you need to make sure you have a unique IP address. Without this, you will run into spamming issues and possibly have your entire campaign blocked. This is regardless of what software you are using.

If you are on an ISP and you share an address, if "Site#1" sends an e-mail blast and gets deemed a spammer, when you go to send yours no matter how pretty, or how high the quality of your list, *you* will now be blocked. This is a barrier to ever having the success rates you need.

An autoresponder campaign only needs to be set up once, and then it will automatically be cycled through by your opt-in leads. Before you get hundreds and thousands of leads, get this set up.

There are two autoresponder methods to choose from:

1. **Third-party.** Examples of this include 1shoppingcart, Infusionsoft, and AWeber. All are good; the best one for you depends on what you need. They all involve a monthly fee to use. Infusionsoft and 1shoppingcart provide extensive affiliate management and shopping cart features. The primary disadvantage to this option is for a start-up, which is costly. AWeber is much simpler, but just handles the database and e-mail communica-tion, not affiliates or payments. If you are just starting out I recommend Aweber.com.

2. **Software located on your ISP.** This is software that
has a unique IP address so nobody else can affect you.
Here you may end up paying as much as option
number one with the increased cost of a good ISP, but
this is a strategic and good long-term option, especially
when your list grows to large numbers (which is what
you want).

For this option I recommend Autoresponse Plus
ARP. You must be on an ISP that has a unique IP (so
you will never be identified and blocked as a spammer,
unless you do something foolish like buy a 100,000
e-mail address list and blast out to it).

The downside of using ARP is that you still need a shopping
cart, affiliate management software, and payment-processing
system. The upside is that it has a low cost for the software
product, they install it for *free*, and you never pay again!

There are no monthly fees so you still have tons of money
left for other things versus a monthly rate-based system. If you
already have a current ISP, check if your IP address is unique,
because if it isn't, you may already be deemed a spammer. Find
out how your hosting provider can make it unique for you.

If you need a shopping cart and want to have your own
affiliate tracking system, then I would recommend the power of
1ShoppingCart.

By getting a system in place to capture the visitors (through
an opt-in system on a landing page), and then applying every
method you can to get traffic flowing to your site, you will
become a successful seller because you will start to control the

markets. You will have interested people at all times to sell yours or other people's products, too, and turn your PC into automated streams of income.

Website Flow When You're Just Starting Out

Sometimes you will have the landing page and autoresponder, but probably not have your own product yet. No worries. Focus on building your database with a landing page, and about 7 to 10 autoresponder messages that educate from the tips in your free gift guide or send the subscriber to your blog or an affiliate program link until your own sales page is ready. You will use the *tracking tag* feature in your autoresponder system to redirect to the next page.

Day 6—Getting Paid While You Sleep

Even though you may not have a sales site yet, you still have to process affiliate payments from your blog or autoresponder activity. Get this established early so that you are ready as soon as your sales page is.

There are two major ways you can go here:

1. Use PayPal to process credit cards and payments.
2. Use a credit card clearinghouse and/or gateway.

The easiest way to process payments is via PayPal. You simply open up a free account at paypal.com and link it to your bank account. Payments are processed based on an online PayPal account balance, or simply accept a credit card if the purchaser doesn't have a PayPal account.

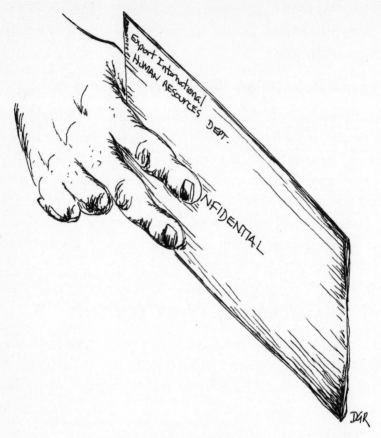

Payment Options

The downside of PayPal is if you have a high-priced ticket item, sometimes the process is not easy if the purchaser is a first-time PayPal user. Another difficult area is if you have a really high balance go into your account at one time (like with a product launch), PayPal can actually hold those funds to investigate what happened with respect to fraud and safety protection. It also offers no ability to directly post to a back-end accounting system.

TIP

If you don't have a product yet, set up a www.paypal.com account to process affiliate payments or small runs. Once you have a product and a launch ready, or do face-to-face sales at events for speaking or books, then you can find out more at www.HowDoIAcceptCreditCardsOnline.com (my keyworded site for Practice Pay).

Whether you need a payment system to accommodate a few orders or one that processes thousands of orders a day, there are various payment systems available to suit your needs.

Two examples of popular payment methods are the Iphone swipe systems for live shows and appearances, and automated credit card authorizations.

My favorite site for the iPhone swipe systems is www.SquareUp.com. It ships you the device for free, and you can be accepting credit cards quickly and easily. It isn't designed for online, but if you are a speaker or attend live events and sell a book, it is a magical way to get your money fast. If you have a smartphone such as an iPhone, you have an instant credit card system.

For automated credit card authorizations you need two pieces to get it working: the credit card payment provider and a gateway to authorize to your bank.

Here are some popular payment types:

- Authorize.Net offers multiple levels of service to process and authorize credit card transactions, including a web-specific option.

- ClearCommerce.com ensures that online transactions are processed in real time. The ClearCommerce engine works with a wide variety of popular storefronts and is compatible with more than 90 percent of credit card processors and merchant banks.

- ICVerify.com is payment processing for many brick-and-mortar merchants.

- PowerPay.biz is one of the largest providers of ecommerce payment solutions in the nation. More than 50 percent of all of the merchants it sets up to process conduct sales over the web.

For Canada, finding the right partner usually involves using a clearinghouse versus a bank. In the United States, most U.S. banks offer Internet merchant accounts and most online transaction providers will support them.

Make certain that your bank accepts Internet merchant accounts and has credit card processors that can connect to available clearinghouses. Ensure that your account handles "Card Not Present" transactions.

If you are an international merchant you'll most likely have to obtain a U.S. merchant account because the vast majority of online transaction providers are located in North America and have limited ability to interact with banks outside. You'll also need to locate a local online transaction provider.

With so many software solutions to choose from, deciding which one is right for you may seem overwhelming, but the more informed you are, the easier it will be.

Online shopping cart software is a cost-effective way to provide you with the ability to display your items for sale, process credit card transactions, and automate the entire ordering cycle.

Your customers can efficiently order 24 hours a day while increasing your credibility on the Internet.

> **Tip**
>
> If you already have a merchant bank account, you may need to upgrade it to an Internet merchant bank account or you won't be protected if anything happens with an online sale.

Payment Cycle

This is a brief list of what happens in the payment cycle. When you grow, eventually you may want to automate the movement of money from this into your accounting system or bank.

- **Build site.** A landing page directs to the sales page. In addition, you select a method of payment processing and integrate these abilities into the site. Once the site is completed the merchant is ready to receive orders from shoppers. If you have just one product, it is the page after the sales page.

- **Visitors place orders.** A visitor places an order, gets sent to the system, and provides personal contact information, including a shipping address.

- **Enter payment details.** Once purchasers enter their personal information they are prompted for the credit card number (or other accepted payment methods). Once the data has been entered, shoppers click on "Confirm Order."

- **Authorize the order.** Once the customer places the order the system will seek approval of the credit card. The system would either submit the credit card details to a payment clearinghouse or directly to the bank's network.

- **Approve or deny.** Once the bank's system receives the transaction authorization back, it approves or denies the order based on the shopper's available credit and status.

- **Return information to store/site.** The approval or denial is then sent back to the store and provided to the shopper. If it was completed, a transaction or order number and receipt is displayed for printing. From start to finish this process usually takes less than eight seconds. When the order is approved, the bank will debit the item on the shopper's credit card, or the funds are transferred into the merchant's bank account.

- **Go to the thank-you page.** Once this cycle has completed you can then send buyers to a page thanking them for the order, to a tell-a-friend page to ask for referrals, or upsell them by directing to another of your products or affiliates (one-time offer), or to get a free CD page.

Then the autoresponders come into play and continue to move buyers through your product from an educational or use perspective, and to move them through the market funnel (gradual steps to increasing products/prices you offer or resell), but we touch more on that later in the book. Let's get one product going with a completed cycle that makes money.

Know Your Power Lies in the List

The most important reason you want to build a list or database of interested people in your product or service is that by creating and controlling markets (owning the list), it makes you the "ruler" with the power.

There are two things Bill Gates knows: one is that the power is in the database, and two, marketing is everything. You may be the best, or know that you're not, but that doesn't matter (yet). What does matter is that you have the list, and that will put you in demand.

Being in business is about asset-building, and your list is the biggest asset you will own. When you capture the visitor you'll be able to sell more at a future date to people who recognize you. Control the list, and you control your ability to have more sales when you want them. Cha-Ching!

We go over how to get traffic to your landing page and into your autoresponder very soon. The key thing to understand here is that **even without a product, and just an inkling of the niche you want to be in, start building your list now**. It may seem backward logic to build a list, and have nothing yet for them, but by doing this you can have a hungry list of subscribers to launch to when you're ready. People are always eager for information, and this prebuild will also let you get familiar with what they really want. This is your chance to survey and ask them, and then build something based on the results.

Having no product will be the least of your worries. If you have a list, people will queue to joint-venture with you (have you send to your list on their behalf, and you get 50 percent of the sales). This is where the real easy money is—push-button cash production. You'll get there, all you have to do is do it.

Product Tip

Even if you have no intention of ever having your own product, you should still *build a database/list*.

The asset for anyone in this industry is the list. This alone becomes a product that will make you a lot of money.

Joint venture partners will give you 50 percent of their profits just for an e-mail blast to your list. It will be the easiest money you will ever make!

A database puts you in the driver's seat.

Chapter 2 Action Plan

- Select your niche.
- Choose domain names.
- Create or get a landing page.
- Create an opt-in offer.
- Select a payment-processing method.

Chapter 3

Turning Prospects into Purchasers

GET PROSPECTS ONLINE BUT MOVE THEM OFF

The Internet has billions of users every day. It's hard to reach that kind of number by calling or by Yellow Page ads, or by any other method. That is why it is such an awesome tool. Having said that, though, you need to really connect with users about what you are offering at the back end. If people have walked through the door, now you can quickly move them to the back end by taking it offline if they have opted-in to any option that promotes a coaching program. Call them. Invite them to a live workshop, or even a webinar. Can you imagine if you converted even just a small percentage of those? They are taking the first step to build a relationship by purchasing and it is your duty now to continue to build on that. Direct contact dramatically increases the speed and number of closed sales.

Especially if you are just starting out, contact them, find out what they are looking for, get personal, and you'll have a good method of keeping people on your list. When you start to have thousands of subscribers, then you can get personal by holding free workshops, webinars, or seminars to meet them, or by providing low-cost events where you encourage them to purchase more advanced programs you offer. Nothing can replace personal contact by you. If you have the time, this is one of the most effective places to spend it. Keep the list you get, and you'll grow faster in the long run.

This section focuses on easy, no excuses why they aren't done, free traffic and page-ranking methods. These methods get people to your site and back links to increase the search engine's awareness of you. This places you higher in a search for the keywords you want. It will focus on free methods, so you don't have to make more investments just yet, until you get a full scope of where you are going, and have a bit of experience generated.

Free Traffic and Page-Rank Techniques

It seems that the holy grail of the Internet is capturing traffic that is relevant to your site. Without traffic you are carrying no real expectations of earning money or customers. When putting your website strategy together you need to remember that it isn't just about the site, but what happens next—the traffic and the conversion of traffic to sales. If you construct a website to sell products, services, or to promote affiliates with the hopes of generating an income, traffic is now of the utmost importance.

Here are 12 *free* ways to get you going. (I expand on larger elements separately.)

1. **Submit your site to search engines.**
   Some of the most popular search engines are:

   www.Google.com

   www.Yahoo.com

   www.DMOZ.org

   www.Bing.com

   www.Excite.com

   www.Lycos.com

   www.MSN.com

You should make sure that you do this as soon as your site is up. Do you know how many people never do this step? In the domain's cpanel or vdeck of your ISP there is often a free utility that will send your domain address to many of the high-ranked search engines. This will help you get into Google and Yahoo! faster as well.

You can do this one search engine at a time or use a service/product or company that will do a global search engine submit for you. It costs, but a site I trust is www.NetMechanic.com.

2. **Signature files.**

Signatures are those little messages that appear at the bottom of your e-mail. Typical examples are your name, e-mail address, company, and position, but in the world of Internet marketing, this is priceless real estate. (Expanded on separately.)

3. **Search engine optimization (SEO).**

SEO or search engine optimization is a fancy way of telling you to make sure that your web pages, titles, meta tags, descriptions, and your page content contain the keywords you want to appear for your particular market. (Expanded on separately.)

4. **Blog.**

This was discussed earlier, but I wanted to put it here again to remind you that the links from your blog to your landing page and other high-ranking pages matter.

5. **Relevant links.**

Many people are saying that links are dead. If you hear that it is because (like myself) we come from the era where link farms, exchanges, and link blasting was rampant. So these types of links are dead, as Google went through Penguin, Panda, and more than 500 algorithm changes to check for spam and duplicate content. Relevant links are the word-of-mouth advertising of the Internet where high-quality content sites link back to yours and vice versa. (This is expanded on later.)

6. **Articles.**

One of the best ways to promote you, your company, and your products or services is to give information away. There are hundreds of free article submission sites and ezine lists on the Internet with tons of sites hungry for free content. In return they make those articles available for anyone else browsing their sites, with a link back to you. It is free exposure. (Expanded on separately.)

7. **Press releases.**

Press releases are a great promotion tool. You can create one, post it on your own site, and submit it to appropriate print, broadcast, and Internet media. If your site is for a general interest audience your options include your local newspaper, and some of your local radio and television stations. If it's a special interest your options include trade publications and broadcast media that focus on some niche area of interest. (Expanded on later.)

8. **Testimonials.**

Testimonial links are great. It may sound trivial but you can get placement on some very big traffic sites just by giving your testimonial about a product you use. (Expanded on separately.)

9. **Post to news/social media groups.**

Post an announcement on all relevant newsgroups. If your website has regional information, post in the general newsgroup for your region. You should limit your postings only to newsgroups, which are designated for commercial announcements. You are trying to build goodwill, so post where and when appropriate.

Social media sites such as YouTube, Facebook, Twitter, LinkedIn, Digg, del.icio.us, ning, Stumbleupon, and hundreds of others are communities where the content is user-powered, and everything is submitted and voted on by the community. These are great sources for dedicated prospects and relationship building. They're becoming a fast and popular way to get your message out, share information, and be connected with large communities of users with like-minded interests. (Expanded on later.)

10. **Your error pages.**

This isn't necessarily traffic, but it can lead to traffic in a situation that would have otherwise been a dead end. Go into your cpanel or vdeck panel for your website, go to your error page management, and make it point to your landing page. That way whenever a bad page is called up, it will simply go straight to your landing page, and get them into your system, that is, Error 400, 404, 403.

11. **Use all regular forms of business communications.**

If you have built your website as a means of generating traffic to your business, be sure also to publicize your website by putting it on your letterhead, your business cards, your invoices, your advertising, and any other form of communication you use regularly to keep in touch with your customers and to pursue new prospects for your business. Don't believe in the axiom, "If you build it, they will come." They won't come if they don't know about it. Your business card especially should be a landing page domain name. Create a specific landing page just for offline promotions that is fast and catchy. Mine is www.just31days.com.

12. **Page ranks.**

Google ranks pages based on back links, content relevancy, and traffic. PageRank is a link analysis algorithm, named after Larry Page and used by Google to assign a numerical weighting based on back links, content relevancy, and traffic.

Here is a guide to those ranks:

0–3: New sites or sites with very minimal links.

4–5: Popular sites with a fair amount of inbound links.

6: Very popular sites that have hundreds of links, many of them quality links.

7–10: Usually media brands (NYTimes.com), big companies, or A-list bloggers.

To find out how your site or anyone else's is doing go to www.prchecker.info.

Day 7—Signature Files

A signature is the file at the bottom of an e-mail and in a world where "There's no such thing as a free lunch," if you use your e-mail signatures effectively, that simply isn't true. Using e-mail signatures is a great way to add to your Internet marketing strategy, and with no cost involved it satisfies a tight budget. Internet marketers and authors use these very effectively.

Here are some signature tips:

- Make sure you are including a signature for each and every e-mail, personal or business, because they work great and are absolutely free.

- Depending on who you are sending an e-mail message to, have multiple signatures you choose from.

- Get your signatures working for you. Be aggressive, and if you have a landing page, drive every e-mail to it so you can capture the e-mail in your autoresponder sales cycle.

- Only have one link for visitors to choose from and make them want to go to it.

If you have never used signatures and are using Microsoft Outlook, go to:

- Tools option on the top menu bar.

- Select Options.

- Select Mail Format.

- Click on the Signatures box at the bottom right hand corner and select New.

- Enter the message you would like to have appear at the bottom of your e-mail.

- Save and make sure the default signature is set to the one you just created.

Here are some examples of effective signatures:

(Your Name)

P.S.—Get a FREE report of the 7 Breakthrough marketing secrets that will catapult your website sales and rocket ride your bottom line.

Go to: www.MarketingSolutionsForBusiness.com

"Save over 50% on your favorite vitamin supplements when you register for a free premium account—today only." LINK>>

Your goal is to get visitors to take action with urgency, otherwise they'll put it off until they forget.

Day 8—Search Engine Optimization (SEO)

SEO or *search engine optimization* is the terminology used to describe the importance of having the keywords you want to appear for your particular market in your web pages. This is done with effective copywriting, and by setting up the HTML body of the page with titles, meta tags, descriptions, headers, and keywords.

When considering your Internet marketing strategy, a free and stable way to get organic (not paid for) traffic from search engines such as Google is to maximize the use of your keywords. Many people rush to Google and Yahoo! and do pay-per-click campaigns (we get into these later), but forget to use the old-fashioned free route of making sure that each web page is maximized to take advantage of the search tools. I have visited many sites and randomly have checked to see if they use them, and they don't. This is a missed, free opportunity at "true ranking" improvement.

It can take a while for search engines to start to notice you and this is where pay-per-click (PPC) programs come into play when you want fast traffic. If you have not optimized your page, though, the free time will never come, and you will always be paying for a good search location. Getting your site listed for the keywords you want on the major search engines is a key to receiving a traffic increase.

When putting together the word content for your page, remember that content is a major difference from appearing on page 1 or page 15 on the searches. Have your keywords and related keywords appear as much as you can, but it's not about repeating the keyword; it is important to have related words as well that tie the topic together.

The next step is a bit more technical, but worth it. This happens inside the HTML code of your web page. At the top of that document there are three lines of code you can add to keyword your title (this is what appears at the top of the address display), your meta description (this is a nice keyword-rich sentence about your site), and the meta keywords (contains your actual 7 to 10 keywords). Make sure you know what your keywords are; this comes before all.

With all four of these elements secured, you will have taken a big step in creating a free relationship with the search engines. This step can take a bit of time if you have to do it after you have already created your website, but if you are just starting out, make sure you do this right away. It should only take a few minutes to create a template and flow it through all of the pages you build. If you are using an HTML editor such as MS-Expression and literally never leave the "Normal or Graphic Mode," you can either try to do it yourself and venture into the

HTML section, or pay to have it done. It shouldn't cost more than $5 to $10 for one to five pages to add just meta tags and title. Go to sites such as www.elance.com or www.guru.com and post a job request. Even this will help if you don't want to invest in copywriting. Another great site is www.fiverr.com. It is really easy to do for people who know what they are doing. An example of what this looks like is: if your market is "Internet Marketing Sales Copy," then you want this to appear in each meta tag and throughout the copywriting.

TIP

TOOL RECOMMENDATION

www.KeywordDensity.com
    It's free—and it helps you to identify how you can improve your keyword density.

If you want to try and add keywords yourself, use this as a guide. Make sure that your blog posts especially are keyword rich.

Editing HTML

- Select HTML or code while the page is loaded in FrontPage, or use an HTML editor, such as HTML-Kit.

- Do not be overwhelmed by all that you will see, just go straight to the top of the page and you should see <html> and <head>. You may even see the title and meta descriptions; if you do, use these and just type what you want in there.

If none of the title or meta tags is there, type everything from below that is missing, inserting your own title, paragraph, and keywords.

<html>

<head>

<title> **Internet Marketing Tips**—What are the Different Types of Websites?</title>

<META NAME="**description**" Content="Get free **Internet Marketing Tips** that will catapult your website sales and rocket ride your bottom line.">

<META NAME="**keywords**" content="**Internet Marketing Tips**, Landing page, squeeze page, Website types, Marketing, Internet Marketing, Marketing Guru, Marketing Sales, Sales and Marketing, wealth building, website sales, marketing tips, online sales">

</head>

- If you do not see the bottom head tag, do not worry, it just means that there is a lot of stuff in between and you do not need to go looking. It will be there. You only need to look at the top four lines of your website page.

Then go to Normal mode to view, to make sure that everything is still okay. Then do a Save As to call it a new name just in case of errors, so that you do not go over a page that is working. You can post to your live site, check it out, make sure it displays, and then rename it to the original name if all is well.

Have fun and take command of the free SEO market, and let the other guys pay for their positions. If you create and upload a one-page placeholder page right now with your keywords and meta tags while you are getting your product done, you could have a Google page-one placement before you launch! I have clients who have been number one in Google before their product even released using this strategy.

Day 9—Link Strategies That Really Work

Links originate from other sites back to yours. Even though the Internet has been through a lot of changes, links are still an important way to generate traffic and maximize the formula of the search engines.

Almost all of the algorithms monitor the links to determine a pages ranking, based on the similarity to your chosen keywords. When you don't have a large advertising budget or even in conjunction with other paid methods, this is a method that is highly recommended as part of an aggressive marketing strategy. In Google Page Rank, Google looks at the popularity of a website and keyword similarity (relevance) in order to determine where it appears in the searches. The desire is page one, the dream is first position, or it could be anywhere after that. It's a work in progress.

A warning comes with links, though: don't link to sites that will pull down the value of your site. Seeking out link farms or paying for bulk links may do more harm than good.

Most links occur in six ways:

1. **Word of mouth.** Referrals from friends, family, business associates, blog postings, and social media site postings by others.

2. **Link exchange program.** This is where you go through the Internet in search of appropriate sites compatible to your niche and offer to list their website if they list yours. Time-consuming, but free.

3. **Affiliate links.** If you have the type of product that can be sold by others where they make a percentage of the sale, make sure they set up a website link back to your site. They will also have a page on your site with a unique identifier so that the sale can be traced back to them. This is a great way to not only increase your links but get your product out there faster.

4. **Articles.** I offer a separate analysis of this method, but the more articles you have out there, the more quickly you get links and gain authority. Remember, though, send them to your landing page.

5. **Press releases.** I offer a separate analysis of this method as well, as it is a great way to rank on some very good sites instantly.

6. **Social media and blogs.** I offer a separate analysis here, but social media, posting comments on blogs, and leaving your website address is a great way to leverage high-ranking sites.

The last thing to consider with links is the quality. This is referring the page rank to a reciprocating site according to the search engines. This is why link farms are not a good way to go. In addition, relevance or niche similarity counts. That way you can move your way to the top of the search engines for your keywords very fast. You can also purchase links, but we stick to the free stuff for now.

Write some sites here that you can leverage for links:

_____

_____

_____

_____

_____

Day 10—Articles

Articles are a great way to put your links into overdrive.

> **Tip**
>
> The rule of thumb is to create 10 articles for your niche, and get them out there fast. Then you can get ready for the viral marketing benefits.

One of the best ways to promote you, your company, and your products or services is to give information away. There are hundreds of free article submission sites and ezine lists on the Internet, with tons of sites hungry for free content. Remember that we spoke earlier about page rank and relevancy. Selecting a good article site (such as www.ezinearticles. com) that has a good ranking will give value back to your site, as long as your article provides readers with useful information and is not for the purpose of selling. This is free exposure for you.

Ezine publishers are also interested in good-quality information to provide to their subscribers. A well-written article results in more free exposure for you because at the end of every article is your *resource information* that contains your website link back to you.

How to Get Articles

- Write them yourself if you have a knack for writing, which will cost you no money at all.

- Subcontract them (ghostwriter) if you aren't comfortable writing them. You can use www.elance.com or www .fiverr.com and have someone write them for you.

- Use private label rights (PLR) to get you started: Buy PLR articles that are prewritten and you can put your name on it. I would recommend changing stuff and at least putting it in your own voice before you send it out, because if you have it, so do others, but it is a great way to get you started.

Once you have an informative article, you can place it on your most applicable article directory. Historically, articles used to be submitted to hundreds at once, creating mass amounts of duplication. Google frowns on that now but the relevant, high-quality link is still worth it.

EXAMPLE

Keywords in Article: 15
Divided by total number of words in article: 750
Multiplied by: 100
Equals: 2%

Here are three article tips:

1. Make sure you created your article with keyword density in mind.

2. Select the directory of your choice, for example, ezinearticles.com.

3. If you want to add something to your blog, add part of it to your blog and link to the full article where you originally loaded it. You will get a link value without content duplication.

Soon you will be getting targeted traffic from visitors who have read your article, found information about you in the resource box, and clicked on your website link that was there. It doesn't take long for the famed "viral effect" of marketing to take place and you've got the traffic you have been waiting for.

A site that lists more than 60 article directories is www .trinityjacobs.com/article-submission-sites.html. Some of the major sites are www.ezinearticles.com, www.articlecity.com, and www .articlebase.com.

You can also type www.google.com and enter "your niche articles" and you can get access to sites that deal specifically with your niche, for example, scrapbooking articles or wealth-building articles.

Have fun, write your articles, get them submitted, and then move on to the next Internet marketing method to get traffic to your site.

Write down your favorite article sites (along with your user ID and password for easy access):

_____

_____

_____

_____

_____

DAY 11—PRESS RELEASES

You can attract more traffic to your site by creating and distributing press releases. A press release is information supplied to reporters or media that is an official statement or account of an event that is specially prepared and issued to make known to the public. It is generally done when you have a newsworthy event such as a new product, website, grand opening, upcoming event, new product feature—but whatever is going on, the key is to write about it, and let everyone know through a press release.

There are two reasons for press releases: (1) to take advantage of the back links; and (2) you legitimately have news and want to get into the major distribution channels. These reasons require slightly different approaches.

For the first option the success of press releases comes back again to links. These are a great way to get links back to your site. You don't get the meaty "author or resource box" that you get in an article, but it can ultimately appear on some really great sites. Any aspect of your business that is interesting or unique should be announced on the Internet. The Internet is one of the largest and easiest ways to get news out there, fast.

Be aware that there is a press release format, although each website has its own instructions that you should follow to increase your chances of being accepted, and being successful. When planning your press release, consider the headline, subheadline, summary paragraph, and the actual body of the article. You want your press release to be interesting—but not sales-oriented—to get the traffic you expect.

The three things for press releases that you need to put your focus on are the headline, the summary, and the keywords.

Your headline is your hook. What is going to pull people in to get them to read it? What can you say that will capture your audience, and take advantage of keywords or news of the day? For example, let's say that the big news story is the Super Bowl. You are promoting your new website. You want to be noticed, so you would consider something like: "Tracy Repchuk's Super Bowl Bet Pays Off."

Then you want to take a look at the summary. This is important from a brief read point of view and keyword insertion. If your keywords are "Internet marketing" and "affiliates," you want them to appear in the summary and have them also capture a reader or media person. The summary appears below the headline, and remember to connect it back to the headline as a supporting statement.

For example: Tracy Repchuk just launched her latest coaching program and with **unemployment at an all-time high** she can now make an introductory offer that she could have only dreamed about with her number one best seller—the Internet marketing bible, *31 Days to Millionaire Marketing Miracles* and affiliate program.

Take note of the tie-in, the keywords, and a tease lead to keep going to the body. Then you write your body giving your full story, and add your Internet address at the end, or separately if requested. Now you're ready to get the word out. You can submit press releases to directories that will broadcast them all over the Internet, along with the information about your company and your website link.

Many of the press releases services charge now, but two that I recommend are free: www.free-press-release.com and www .prlog.com.

Popular Fee-based Services

- www.PRWEB.com

- www.i-newswire.com

- www.send2press.com

- www.ereleases.com

For the second option, a legitimate news story, with the ability to provide value to the audience of the media carrier, needs to be written differently—with the hook being what is in it for the audience. If you have some truly amazing news story, major award win, or something that is really worth getting out there in an enormous way, then you should go to a paid distribution service. The service is well worth it, and your link and traffic will explode once it viral markets around the world to a possible 40,000 sites.

As an aside, if you absolutely can't write a press release but really want to get one out there, go to places such as www.elance .com or www.fiverr.com and post a job request. For a very low cost, you can get one written for you.

Day 12—Testimonials Speak Louder

Giving testimonials is free. If you have used someone's product and like it, go to the company's site and see if it accepts testimonials. You will know it does if there are some posted. If there are no postings, ask the company if it would like yours to post on its site. This can get you many back links on some good sites, for free. Don't underestimate your opinion, and start searching for opportunities to get your face on some great sites. Try to get at least three. By appearing on other sites you may even start to be seen as an authority in your own field. Just make sure that your full name and website link are part of it, and include a head shot. Also, if you have read a book and bought it through an online source, post a review/testimonial, which gets you noticed as well. And get as many as you can, with name, location, picture, and even better, video.

Day 13—Social Media Squared

Social media is no longer an element you can ignore, because for every post you do, the power can be squared if shared in the eyes of Google and your fans. Today's technology is referred to as *Web 2.0*, which is a term used to take aspects of technology and describe them in relation to how they advanced from a prior version. For example, social media comes under Web 2.0, as does blogging. Web 1.0 technologies would be a personal website versus Web 2.0, which is called a *blog*. Page views versus cost per click. It is the sophistication advancement that places it under a new heading. Before you wanted something to be "sticky," now you want it to be RSS (real simple syndication) fed. Before it was the encyclopedia online, now it's Wikipedia. These are examples of such a migration.

Social media naming is part of your brand. For example, if you are the brand then your name should be what you secure. And don't put spaces or change it for each one. You should secure the same name across the board. If your brand is a company, then secure that name across the board but test in Twitter first. Twitter is the shortest so you want whatever you can get there to be carried along for consistency.

Below are some sites you must get an account for, and remember to keep your name consistent.

- www.Facebook.com
- www.LinkedIn.com
- www.YouTube.com
- www.Twitter.com
- www.Pinterest.com
- www.Instagram.com
- https://plus.google.com/
- www.Digg.com
- www.Stumbleupon.com
- www.Delicious.com

There are thousands of others. It is the fastest-growing area for distributing your message, and will be an area of exploding power. Everything is submitted and voted on by the community, giving the general public the ability to determine trends, successes, and allows each person to voice his or her opinion and make a difference.

Like search engines, Web 2.0 sites are controlled by custom algorithms. Hailed as "user-driven social content," its front page is often populated with the items that have been voted most newsworthy by the community. Web 2.0 groups can provide you a wealth of traffic, interest, and potential customers, particularly if the social group is within your area of expertise or niche. For the most part, social groups are a relatively untouched area for businesses, partly because they have no real idea of the potential that sits within the groups. A few pioneering corporations are jumping into the water to see if it is worth their efforts and using it as a grassroots campaign to build word-of-mouth frenzy and buzz. Certainly until this is detected it might produce some short-term effects, but given the nature of this platform I am hoping any insincerity is discovered and replaced with honest opinions and feedback.

Social groups are niches right at your fingertips of any-where from 20 to more than 1,000 people with a tremendous potential for the growth of your business. From around the world they meet, talk, and socialize with each other for a variety of reasons. They are a fast and popular way to get your message out, share information, and be connected with large commu-nities of users with like-minded interests, while providing excitement and possible profit. This is where your audience is, meeting quite often daily. An example would be if you were an expert in the niche of direct marketing, you will definitely have no problem finding a social group that caters to only direct marketers. By becoming a member of the group you will have opened a new avenue of promotion for your business, products, and services.

Establishing Yourself as a Niche Expert

Because members of social groups are generally very close, they would be more apt to come to you for products and services as a member than they would a nonmember. For the most part, social group members believe in supporting and promoting their own. By becoming a member and talking with the social group about various topics, you have the ability to establish yourself as an expert in your niche by offering advice, guidance, and information. You could also volunteer to write an article for the group or volunteer to give a presentation or teleseminar. The key is to solve a problem, provide a solution, and promote yourself as an expert.

Getting started is not hard. In fact it may be easier than any other method you have tried, particularly if you become an active member of that group. You can start out with just simply mentioning your business, products, or services, as well as your website through normal conversation between members. Once you have established yourself with the group and are ready to start taking advantage of the promotional possibilities, you could start with offering a special discount or free product specifically for members. This is a great way to increase your traffic, as well as sales. The key here though is to not start off by promoting yourself, but by helping people and in time the introduction of your services will be natural and welcomed.

The most popular sites are:

- www.YouTube.com
- www.LinkedIn.com
- www.Facebook.com
- www.Twitter.com
- www.plus.google.com
- www.Craigslist.com

If you have a niche and would like to join a social group, just go to www.google.com and type in (your niche) social group, and at least one should appear. To secure *your name* across almost 100 sites, go to www.namechk.com.

Two steps are required to secure your name:

1. Enter your name with *no* spaces, for example, Tracyrepchuk.

    If you leave a space, it will look for tracy-repchuk and then the master page can still can be taken later by someone else. It's like not getting the .com in a domain.

2. Then go to each site, and secure the name, or outsource someone to do it. If you have kids, pay them to do this. :)

    Use same e-mail, user ID, and password for as many as you can.

Use http://hootsuite.com when you want to send a post to many social media sites at once.

BlogTalkRadio/Ustream TV

Two great technologies that have become a staple in the industry to communicate with others and get the message out fast are BlogTalkRadio and Ustream TV.

Both are easy to use and get you syndicated across the Internet to millions of people in minutes. It is the new era in audio and video distribution (advanced version of podcasting and YouTube). In minutes you can be the host of your own radio or TV show online. In fact, I have three of them, and celebrated the 100th show put on by a group of us called *The Fab 5*. If are you looking for a way to be heard around the world, attract traffic to your sites, increase your profile, gain access to interview other well-known people, and require no skills whatsoever except the ability to talk—then www.blogtalkradio.com and www .Ustream.TV are for you!

Get started on your own show, and you'll also create a way for you to get easy content for giveaways, products, bundles, or promotion.

Facebook and Fan Pages

Facebook is one of the most popular social media platforms with more than 1 billion people actively using it. It is a force to be employed for communication, relationships, promotion, publicity, and power.

I have made a lot of money on Facebook, but none of it from selling. It is in the relationships I created with people that I met.

If you aren't on or using Facebook yet, or think it's a waste of time—do it now by following these eight steps:

1. Go to www.Facebook.com.

2. Click on sign up (in the future you'll just log in) and enter all information it requests.

3. Finish the registration by confirming an e-mail.

4. Try to get your own name as your Facebook page, for example, www.Facebook.com/TracyRepchuk.

   - Go to www.Facebook.com/username/.

   - Check if your name is available. If not, get something as close as you can.

   - You use this for a Fan Page as well. It might sound weird to you—but build a business fan page, too.

5. Once you're in your record, select Profile and fill out any information you wish to be known.

6. Make sure you add your photo. This is very important.

7. Find friends, either by joining regional groups, or searching friend names.

8. Select Save or Done when appropriate.

And what do you do now? Post a message on your wall in the box where it says Write Something. There are tutorials on Facebook, there are YouTube videos you can watch to help you familiarize what you do, and how to get the most benefit out of Facebook.

I use it to create relationships, and from that I get money-making opportunities. I use it to promote webinars and special offers. I don't sell, sell, sell *ever* on Facebook. You will lose friends fast if you do. Here are a couple of examples.

My Facebook (5,000 friend limit):
www.Facebook.com/tracyrepchuk

My Facebook Fan Page (open and unlimited):
www.facebook.com/TracyRepchukFan

Twitter Tricks

Twitter is a tool that asks one question: What Are You Doing? and you answer that and anything else in 140 characters or less. I am not sure it is serving much purpose unless you are a celebrity; however, I use it to drive traffic/subscribers to a landing page. It is how I list build. I do not use it to sell, but I do promote when I am appearing live somewhere, or have a webinar/teleseminar.

One of the most fascinating things about Twitter is the tools there are. This is massive list-building power when you combine the target audience of Twitter with the data capture of your landing page. I have many followers, I do nothing to get them, and I send them to my own database via a landing page. The key to remember about social media accounts is that the followers aren't yours so it is important not to just leave them there, but to get them into your own funnel.

Four Steps to Setting Up an Account

1. Go to www.Twitter.com.

2. Click Get Started/Join

3. Type in your full name and if available as a Unique User Name. If it is gone, make a slight change like you would your blog name.

4. Create a password, follow the remaining instructions, and then select friends to follow from your own systems (if you want to), then from a suggested list of common tweeters.

Then watch my video and do a few tweets just to get your feet wet. It isn't critical until you have your landing page ready.

Twitter Tools That Help You

- This is for any time you need to reduce a website name and allows you to track results: www.bitly.com

- Twitter directory, more than 2,000 apps: http://twitdom .com/

- Twitter submitter: www.bufferapp.com

- Delete people who are not following you back: http://dossy .org/twitter/karma/

- Twitter manager: www.TweetDeck.com
- Twitter blog: www.TwitWall.com
- Track your stats: http://twittercounter.com/

Twitter Video to Help You Get a List Built   My account is www.Twitter.com/TracyRepchuk. I created this video to help new people to Twitter to learn how to use it. Here is free direct access to it: www.TwitterTweetsandMore.com.

Google+ Your Profile

Google+ is a relative newcomer to the game of social media but with a name like Google it doesn't take much to change the game. Google has combined the power of other platforms and created an environment that is ideal for businesses. Make sure you add this to your portfolio.

If you want to create a Google+ Business Account go to www.google.com/+/business.

Follow the instructions and set up your account.

These are the features you want to get familiar with and take advantage of:

Circles: One of Google+'s key innovations is that it allows you to separate your customers and suppliers into different groups, which is perfect if you market to multiple niches.

Ripples: A cutting-edge analytical tool that helps you understand how your business is being viewed by your customers and potential customers.

Hangouts: The teleconferencing facility allows you to hold meetings, meet with customers, and even host online seminars.

Translate: This is the World Wide Web. So, if you have limited yourself to English so far, here is an instant way to widen your reach—massively.

Messenger: This facility takes sending texts to a whole new level and is perfect now that mobile Internet marketing has taken off big time.

Research each of these—I am sure there is a YouTube video demonstrating the power of what these are—the key is that you need to start familiarizing and using these now.

Google+ is getting ready for its plan for Internet domination, and with $200 billion in its pockets, it will probably succeed and you want to be at the forefront of this effort.

LinkedIn Leverage

LinkedIn is a social networking site designed specifically for the business community. The goal of the site is to allow registered members to establish and network with people they know and trust professionally.

I have been on LinkedIn since 2007, and if you are a business, speaker, author, coach, entrepreneur, and provide a product or service, you need to be on LinkedIn.

This is where the "professionals" hang out. This is where your target audience probably is, and your possible marketing partners. I have made the most money from connections here either by attracting them as clients, or connecting to partners.

To open a new account go to www.LinkedIn.com. Follow the directions to create an account. Once you have created it, connect to me and see some of the things I say and have done as you set up your profile.

Here is my LinkedIn: www.LinkedIn.com/in/TracyRepchuk.

Day 14—Autoresponders: Why They Work

Without autoresponders, the dreams of making money while you sleep wouldn't be possible. Can you imagine selling thousands of products online without a shopping cart to process the orders, record payment, and in some cases ship it, or prepare the documents? That was overwhelming before the advent of catalogs and shopping carts.

Data collection, lead collection, and cost per acquisition (CPA) systems are similar concepts in that they can lead to a large influx of visitors. Imagine getting 270,000 visitors and you were expected to build a relationship with them individually. As much as people want that volume, without the proper systems in place it would crush your company. The purpose of the autoresponder is to help you manage your leads, effectively communicate on a personal level, and do it all while you are doing other things.

Autoresponders work in two ways:

1. They provide a way to communicate on a one-to-many scale, while giving you the ability to focus as if each visitor was getting one-on-one personal attention.

2. They provide a mechanism to automatically give information in digestible chunks to the consumer, allowing them to make an informed decision at the pace they can cope with.

The key is to have as your foundation a way to capture all of the traffic and interested prospects, respond to them continuously bit by bit, and build a relationship until they are comfortable with you and your company. All the while you provide them with information and reasons to get in touch, with helpful tips and advice about what you have. You are building a relationship so that eventually visitors feel that they know you, trust you, like you, and buy from you. And when you have a product or service that delivers what it promises, you have a customer for life.

Direct marketers have known for years that it takes an average of seven times of contact with a new prospect before that person becomes a customer. That is an alarming statistic given that the frequency most salespeople will call or someone will visit your site is once. That means the industry is falling short of making the sale by a startling six follow-ups. The good news is that autoresponders save the day and automate the grunt work of repeating the same thing to all people who come to check out your product or service in such a way that they feel like it is personal, one-on-one, and that they are getting vital information to the point that they can make an informed decision. This works because it is the least expensive sales rep you will ever have; working 24/7, with no breaks, no vacations, and loves to get to know your prospects.

Now the beauty of this is that you have created the messages, delivered the pitch in a heartfelt reach to your prospects, embraced their desires, focused on their benefits, and you only had to do it once. You can reach many prospects with just one effort. An autoresponder is a vital tool for your Internet marketing company, so choose wisely, learn and master it, and think of it as a staff member who can do a lot of work for you while you sleep.

Autoresponders—Telling Your Story

Autoresponders are the tools you use to easily and effectively communicate with thousands of people from just one effort. You create it once, and it continues to work for you, automatically. The initial sale is simply the front end, and the big payoff will come at the back end, so every sale is a possible windfall, and the relationship building in between is crucial.

Autoresponder writing is an art that intelligently weaves your story and experiences with the information that you provide along with your sales pitches. It is written as you would say it to one person as if he or she were directly in front of you. This includes where you came from, how you got to where you are, things that are happening in your life—this is no place to be shy or reserved. You are talking to real people at the other end via text, so if you want to stir them to act, or relate to you, or care about you, you have to let them in as far as you can. This is the *key* to successful communication using an automated medium.

In the industry, there is a general standard with the follow-up cycle that we go through later that allows you to put together one of the most powerful passive income streams on earth.

Some will purchase and then move to another level in your autoresponder tracking system (market funnel covered later), and the game continues, only here the offers can be sent more frequently because of the marketing funnel level of trust.

Then within that normal cycle you make sure to insert a broadcast sales campaign or product push each week to your prospects, which is separate from your automated cycle. These are the act-now special offers.

Over the next year visitors should receive an average of one message a week and buy more and more from you if the campaigns are structured successfully. This is where autoresponders really help your marketing funnel to produce hot, hyperactive purchasers of your product or service. Best of all, it is all automated and works while you sleep, play, and grow your business.

There are three things to remember:

1. The money is in the follow-up, and that is done by using your autoresponder cycle.

2. If you aren't a writer or a salesperson, and this isn't something you want to do, hire somebody to do it—because it is a very important part of the success of your campaign. Be sure to check out www.elance.com or www.guru.com or www.easyoutsourcingnow.com and post what you are looking for, and someone else will do it for you.

3. Share your story. Get personal in your e-mails. Let people know what you have been through, done, didn't do and should have, bare your soul and reveal your motivations to what you do, and why. Getting personal with your prospects is a great way to let them know they can trust you and you'll tell them anything. No matter what you say, somebody will relate to it.

You need to set up an autoresponder cycle for each product, each service, and each level of everything you do. But remember, just once, and it will work for you forever.

Autoresponders—Success Cycles

Once you have the landing page, your niche, the opt-in, and the autoresponder, now it's time to get busy with your autoresponder plan. This is where the relationship building starts. When considering your Internet marketing strategy make sure you understand that the money is in the follow-up.

Autoresponder communication is broken down into two types. One is your automated stream serving as your sales force, repeating your message down along the line. The other is called a *broadcast*. This is done when you have a time-sensitive message that needs to go to everyone now. We look at both types.

In the beginning you need to get familiar with your list fast. There are two schools of thought here: one is an interval system like the one I outline below, the other is simply sending an e-mail every day for 10 days, then switching to once a week. Both are effective. It comes down to which one you are comfortable with.

Regular Sending—Automated Communications

SEND = "IMMEDIATE" (Welcome): In this e-mail you welcome users, thank them, and either provide a link to any reports or gifts you used to entice them, or give them a tip or other information so they are excited about the next steps.

SEND = NEXT RUN: After you have welcomed them, the next run is about an hour later and starts to provide them with some meat and potato content, or the first tip if it is in a series.

SEND = INTERVAL: 1 (this is one day after last): Again, one day after last run, you give them more content. You're getting them familiar with who you are while it is still fresh in their mind that they opted-in.

SEND = INTERVAL: 2 Days Later (than the last): Give them more content, let them know they can reach you if they have questions, give them a tip, something to keep them interested and connected to you and your list.

SEND = INTERVAL: 2 Days Later (than the last): Now you can pitch to them, gently and delicately, woven in with your own personal anecdotes, a story, and the benefits you want them to have with your product. You are offering your product to help them. Let them know you care, and you have something that can help.

SEND = INTERVAL: 5 Days (after the last one): More content, tips, benefits, whatever you want to say to keep in touch.

SEND = Interval: 7 Days (after the last one): Time to sell again, and with a message of: urgency, act now, special offer, don't wait. Start to get them trained to reacting quickly to your e-mails, that way when you start the broadcast cycle they know that they are time-limited, act now offers.

Continue to add "messages" until you have achieved what you want, which is a sale that puts them on the next level of the marketing funnel.

Broadcast Message   This is a cycle that is not part of the regular series, but is inserted weekly for a specific purpose. This is where you tell them about a great new product or service, either yours or an affiliate product you represent and sell. This is your direct, targeted, specific sales push, with the intention of converting a portion of your database to purchasers, and the next level of your marketing funnel.

Autoresponders are your automated sales team willing to sell over and over again for you, for as long as you want, for free and the really great part is, that is just a fraction of what they can do.

In addition to your regular cycle, autoresponders can also:

- Recruit affiliates for you and help to create a team of sales reps with deep networks of new prospects.

- Serve as a training program after the purchase, offering set-up tips, tricks, common questions encountered, ways to maximize what buyers have purchased, and show them that you care even after they have bought.

- Ask for feedback or request a testimonial. Either way you get something that will help your company—whether it is suggestions of ways you can improve, or a testimonial that you can use in promotions.

- Put together a few resources of products that help buyers, preferably something you are an affiliate for. That way you can sell to them automatically and help them and you at the same time.

- Use autoresponders to conduct surveys. If you have a product or service you are considering or want to get some solid questions answered, get a survey done once in a while. Find out from the people who bought from you before what would interest them now. You can get a free survey creator and results generator at www.surveymonkey.com.

You can send out new article announcements to everyone, or send them to your blog when you have a new posting. You can constantly and easily keep in touch, before, during, and after the sales cycle.

Google AdSense Advice

Google AdSense is a platform on which advertisers pay a set amount (through bidding) for their ads to rank for specific keywords. These ads are then displayed on web pages that are keyword-optimized for that topic. You have the ability to set up pages that give permission for these ads to be placed on your site, and get paid a percentage of the "click-through" price when selected by a visitor.

You have to hand it to Google—it has revolutionized the advertising model by combining its pay-per-click formula with themed advertising, and in the process not only generate enormous profits for itself, but also helps many Internet marketers build multiple streams of income on automatic. It is a win-win-win combination. The underlying framework is quite simple. Publishers/advertisers pay Google on a pay-per-click basis for their target keywords. Google, after taking a percentage as revenue, pays the remainder to the website owner. You are getting paid for your website real estate whenever someone clicks through on the advertiser's link on its website.

The rates on some websites are astonishing and there are keywords that pay as much as $50 or more per click-through. You will need to balance the payout with the demand for that keyword. Nothing is worse than optimizing for a keyword that only gets a 100 searches a month, no matter how much it pays. Google AdSense can consume an entire study in itself, but we'll get familiar with it enough to get it on your site and earn you money. Then you can delve deeper and learn how to manipulate ads and chase keywords through materials from gurus such as Joel Comm.

Eight Steps to Building and Maximizing Passive Streams of Income

1. Go to Google.com. Sign in under your account. The username is the e-mail address you used to sign up. If you set up a blogger.com account earlier, use this to activate AdSense, and later AdWords.

2. Once logged in, click on the "AdSense Set Up" tab.

3. Review the types of advertisements available to you.

   A. "AdSense for Content": You can display Google AdSense word advertisements on your website.

   B. "AdSense for Search": You can offer your visitors relevant searches and get paid to give them that free service.

   C. "Referrals": You can earn more money off the AdSense program by referring people to Google.

4. Click on the "AdSense for Content" option.

5. You now need to look over the selection of advertisements that you need to post to your site or blog. For this example, we choose "Link Units."

   Click the Continue button.

   Choose the format. You will see a drop-down menu to your left. Click on it.

   Review the sizes. You can either choose horizontal or square ads in various sizes. (Large rectangle and leader board are best; 728 x 90 at the top.)

   Choose the number of links you want to appear on your code. You may choose 4 or 5.

   Choose your color. Choose something that complements your site's natural base colors. See the drop-down menu to the right. Click on the down arrow.

(Blank/white is best, no border. You do not want it to stand out as an ad.)

Click on a menu spot to "test" the colors. If you look to your bottom left you will see a box that is a "Google AdSense" box. As you change selections from the drop-down menu, this box will change colors.

6. Choose an alternate advertisement in case there are no relevant advertisements that come up. My suggestion is to put your favorite business opportunity URL in the ad space. Try and make more off the customers that are present versus providing a default free placement of a not-for-profit ad.

Click Continue on the screen.

7. You need to choose your advertisement channels through this section. Click on the "AdSense for Content" area and then click on the "URL channel."

8. If you want to eliminate your competition from your website, insert their links in the area called "Competitive Ad Filter." Click continue.

Get your AdSense code. Copy and paste it into notepad and save it to your desktop for safekeeping. If you need to see the entire advertising page again, click the "Single Page" link. This allows you to edit or create other versions of the advertisement.

Keyword density is:

Total times keyword (#) appears in the document divided (/) by total number of words (#) multiplied (*) by 100 (100) equals (=) Keyword Density of Article (%)

Its physical equivalent looks like this: 15/750 * 100 = 2%

A free automatic tool is www.KeywordDensity.com.

TIP

Copy the AdSense code to a web page that has been search engine–optimized to Keyword Density of 2 to 5 percent to ensure that your advertisement actually produces relevant results.

Remember to add this code to your blog as well. Back up the template or do a Save As to test, open the template option and insert the code. For my blog, I put it down the right-hand margin below my picture. Test this, and when it displays fine, do this to your actual template that gets published. This will go through every page, including your archives. Cha-Ching!

Top Five Ways to Network Offline

Networking is a skill that once mastered becomes a way to attract people to your business, products, seminars, anything, in an offline world. If there has been a successful action that I have done, that has been getting out from behind my computer and going to events in my field. Attend workshops, seminars, and definitely shows. If you want joint venture partners later, they come primarily from these places. While you are at these events, you want to optimize your time. Even when you're at an event not necessarily related to your industry, you would be surprised at who you can meet in the real world. With most of our efforts going into getting traffic online, it's easy to forget we actually have offline methods, too. (Remember, from the olden days.)

Networking is a breeze for some, and torture for others. It truly involves putting yourself out there, letting others get to know you, and then simply waiting for the reaction. It is this diverse reaction that causes people to be adverse to networking and taking advantage of this critical part of the business cycle. Networking simply involves meeting and interacting with others to improve the status of yourself, your business, and your product or service.

Let's take a look at the five ways to network so that it becomes a part of your lifestyle.

1. **The initial greet**.

    Remember that when you meet someone they are just like you. They are there to meet people, get contacts, grow their business, and you are just as good a candidate to them as they are to you, so be confident. Have good eye contact, a firm handshake, introduce yourself, ask them what they do—make it about them, what can you do to serve them, and then you can see where you fit in to what they do. You have the advantage of custom tailoring the conversation to what you can provide for them. Keep your body language loose and relaxed, be comfortable, and be yourself. Get passionate about what you can do for them, and leave them with a lasting impression.

2. **Your goal for each person**.

    Because you have managed to "cause" the conversation, gain the advantage of hearing about people first so you can now speak to suit their needs. This also gives you time to think about your goal for each person you meet. Is this a possible client, a potential partner, a great marketing contact—whatever that person does, he or she can probably help you in some way, even if it isn't for the purpose you approached the person. Be flexible, and keep each person in mind for something.

3. **Becoming a networking butterfly**.

When you are at a networking or social event, time is money. Once you have swapped cards, exchanged information, and you have understood what the goal for this person is, it is time to move on. You need to spread your wings, politely depart, and meet someone else. The key is in the follow-up after the event where you can spend oodles of time talking, but right now you have a mission, and that is to meet as many people as possible in the time allocated. The relationship building comes later. You can glance around and preselect the next person who seems available, thank your current prospects for their time, tell them it was a pleasure meeting them, and that you'll contact them when you get back to your office next week. Good eye contact again, firm handshake, and move to your next person. Don't worry about leaving them standing there—the point is to not hang out with people who are afraid to work the room, and you work it. That they'll remember.

4. **The money is in the follow-up**.

This is the time where you take all of your business cards, get organized, know who was good for what, sort them in a database such as BigContacts.com, or simply e-mail them and invite them to collect a free gift and opt-in to your autoresponder system. Then plan your strategy. If they were possible clients, call these people first. Have a scripted message if you need one to make sure that your goal is met, and have another one in case you get voicemail that you can pleasantly expound. Then keep working them until your objectives are achieved. Remember, this is just like the networking event—you have many calls to make, so once you have the next action step for them or yourself, it is time to move on.

5. **Growth and expansion**.

Networking is a vital part of your growth and expansion whether you do it at a live event or set up a strategy where you can do it online through various technologies such as landing pages, autoresponders, and teleseminars. Make sure you take care of all the people you meet, keep in touch through newsletters or calls and e-mail, and good management of these relationships will make a significant contribution to your business.

As soon as you can, add them to your autoresponder system and let the automatic relationship building begin.

For this step, though, never do it automatically even if people gave you their card—send a separate e-mail reminding them how they met you, and inviting them to join your "community" or get a free gift, or go here to keep in touch.

Overall, if you are confident in what you are offering, just follow the five steps and you'll become a networking pro in no time at all. Your best connections will happen outside of your computer, so add it to your plan to get out at least once a month, even if it is to a Chamber of Commerce meeting or local meetup .com group.

Chapter 3 Action Plan

- Address and implement each traffic strategy.
- Create your Facebook page.
- Create your Google+ page.
- Create your LinkedIn page.
- Create your Twitter page.
  (Try to keep these *all* the same.)
- Write five autoresponders for your first visitor from your landing page.

CHAPTER **4**

Catapulting to Product Profits

S pecial note: To give you examples of each type of product, I send you to my site and the products I have so you can examine them. I am not sending you to "buy it." The reason this book is filled with my stuff is that I do everything I talk about and I teach by example—so please know it is for evaluation *only*!

Day 15—Rapid Product Creation in Five Easy Steps

Creating a product, believe it or not, is the easy part. You have researched your niche, combined your passion with your skills or recognized a market ripe for profit, selected your product type, now you just need to do it. If at this point you are still petrified at the thought and horror of creating your own product, then you can do a couple of things to get a jumpstart on this step.

The Top Five Easy Steps to Get a Product

1. **Become an affiliate.** Sell other people's stuff. Just remember to have a landing page to capture visitors before you turn them over. You'll want them eventually, and the list *is* a product. You can find many affiliate products to choose from on www.Clickbank.com. The key is that this is not a long-term strategy, and it is only buying you time while you build your own product.

2. **Use a ghostwriter.** Say what you know into a recording device and use someone from www.guru.com or

www.elance.com to transcribe, rework, and turn it into an ebook for you. You can do the same for a book, but this will cost more, and you need to add a professional edit cycle and book graphics.

3. **Get resell or master resell rights.** Buy resell rights to an ebook or master resell rights to an ebook, and you can sell either one for full profit. A great site is www .masterresalerightsforsale.com.

4. **Interview.** If you don't feel like you have anything worth listening to or saying yet—find someone who does, and interview them. Repeat this a few times, get it transcribed, work in a few anecdotes and personalize it a bit, and you have yourself a great ebook, book, or audio. This was the concept behind *Conversations with Millionaires*, which became a number one international best seller. I do this and give them away, but many people create whole membership sites around interviews, such as www.InterviewsForYourLife.com (the first interview I did—free access—was so bad I am embarrassed now). I want to hit you hard with this message that I learned from my mentor six years ago— "You don't have to get it right, you just have to get it going." Just do what you have to and get your dreams going.

5. **Sell or enhance public domain stuff.** Once something has expired under current copyright laws, you can get it for free, and sell it, modify it, do what you want with it. Go to the site that holds expired public domains (www .Gutenberg.org) and you have an instant product. This is where classics such as *Think and Grow Rich* and *Science*

of Getting Rich came from. Wouldn't you have loved to have been the one to find these and take them to market and millions?

Now, it is time to create.

Keep your product creation thoughts open as to how you can build and integrate with each for a full product range. Depending on your sales skills, you can also cut out any number of the "market funnel" stages, and sell the premium package directly. My only advice on rushing from an intro to a premium product is the learning skills needed by your purchaser to perform the tasks and the steep learning curve that may be involved. The same goes if you are a first-time purchaser going for the top level. Read what will be required of you before you jump in with both feet.

DAY 16—SELECT YOUR PRODUCT TYPE

From the earlier chapters you should now have your niche, and the focus you want to take with your product. Now you want to select the medium where your product will appear. Internet marketing is a gold mine for digital products, but the concepts work for a service or tangible product as well (it's just more work). Once you have selected your *core focus* such as a solution to someone's problem, or an obsession, you can add products that revolve around that. This gives you concentrated income streams, and starts to create the blueprint for your million-dollar design. I give you lots of samples of my products—not so you rush out and buy, but so you can see how I set it up and promote them. In fact don't buy them. I don't want to be accused of rigging this game in my favor. Just study them.

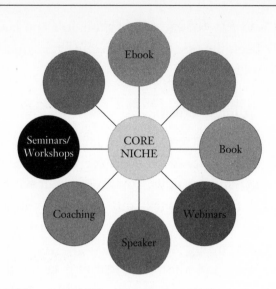

Figure 4.1   Millionaire by Design Chart (MBD)

Figure 4.1 is the chart I use to teach my upper-level clients (which was taught to me by my coaching mentor). It makes Internet marketing easy—just choose your core focus and take that same information through to each of the product types. You just need to know a small amount of information about a topic and keep recycling it through each area.

You can come in from any direction, any starting point, just take the same information and create different options of distribution and price point.

Creating an Ebook

This is pitched as being one of the easiest and fastest ways to put together a product. You simply write what you know into a word processor, format it, print it in PDF, and post it for sale. However, it does require you to write it, format it, and pretty it up, especially if you are going to put *your name* on it. To me, *you are your brand*, so despite what you may have heard, quality does matter.

Create and Ebook in Five Steps

1. Write what you know into a word processor.

2. Format it. Add pictures, footer, header, table of contents (use an outsourcer if you don't want to do this part).

3. Print it in PDF (www.cutepdf.com).

4. Get a cover page made and post it for sale (www .EbookGraphicsDoneForYou.com).

5. Create a website to sell it from and promote it. Creating the ebook is the easy part. The effort starts with selling it—as this is where you need to create the sales page and autoresponder messages that go with it.

Once you have sold the ebook you can upsell the purchasers and offer to sell them resell rights. This gives them the right to not only read it for themselves, but sell it and keep all of the profits. Then, you can do it again. Offer to sell them master resell rights, which gives purchasers the ability to sell the ebook with the resell rights they bought in the previous option, to others. They will make money, and it becomes an expanded profit stream for you as well.

One ebook can create three products that range in price from $47 to $197 to $397. How cool is that!

EBOOK TIP

If you are not a fast typist, simply speak your ebook into a microphone and record it in an MP3 format, and get it transcribed into Word, then print to PDF.

You can download free PDF software (www.cutepdf.com), which will take what is in your document and print it to a PDF just like it was printing to a printer. Very easy, and you have your ebook. Graphics are a *very* important element of your product design, so don't neglect them. Come out of the gates looking professional—you have one chance to make a first impression.

It is part of the ebook process that may cost you depending on how elaborate you want to be. You can purchase software or services to easily create your ebook covers. You can also search in Google, or check these two (make it look good though—first impressions count):

1. www.EbookGraphicsDoneForYou.com

2. www.fiverr.com (for $5, find a graphics guy)

For my journey, I created the book first, then after years of sales, added the ebook. I made more money on the ebook, but it kills the book sales sometimes as people like instant download, especially now with Kindle or Nook. I add this as an aside—the formatting and rules are different in the creation of a Kindle book, but if you're going the ebook route, to increase your exposure investigate having a Kindle version. It becomes a legitimate Amazon book then, and if done right, it goes to bestseller and you have new bragging rights. The negative part— most people sell Kindle books for *cheap* and ebooks for a lot more. My ebook sold for $47. If I created a Kindle version, it probably would have sold for $7.99 tops. That is a volume game.

Creating a Book

The route I started if you look at the Millionaire by Design chart earlier in the book (MBD) was a full book—and I'm not necessarily recommending that unless you have two things in place. **(1) A back end.** The book is not the money maker. You are using the book to raise your profile, and to generate leads for your big product such as coaching. It is a powerful business card. It took me from obscurity to number one on Amazon to getting noticed by people in an aggressive industry in weeks. It is the front end of your funnel. **(2) A strong marketing plan.** I worked on marketing as much as I wrote to prepare for the launch. Even if you have a publisher, they publish. Your job is to promote and sell it. So a book isn't a magic pill that will take you from obscurity to best seller to recognized expert. You do that. You are just using the book as a tool. This is a fantastic product if you want to quickly increase your exposure and perceived value in an industry, especially if you become an Amazon bestseller. But if you expect it to make you money, your model may be flawed and shortsighted. To get started, use the same format as an ebook for content, but properly format and get a professional cover, editing, and formatting. This is costly, but you cannot skimp on this step or it might not be worth what you thought.

To self-publish go to www.CreateSpace.com (this is an Amazon subsidiary with a ton of information on the whole process).

Creating an Audio Product

Audio products are a very easy route. Just say what you know, or interview someone who knows it, and post it for sale. Making an audio product is even easier than making an ebook, but ebooks sell better in most cases. Sample: www.Quantum LeapSecrets.com.

You can create it for use on an iPod, a podcast, digital download, or an audio CD. You can purchase products that make this really easy, or if money is tight, you can follow these steps and do it practically for free.

Try this: www.FreeAudioSoftwareForAll.com.

If it doesn't work or isn't free, go through the five manual steps:

1. Get a microphone or phone headset ($20). Most computers come with a sound card, so all you need to do now is get a microphone or headset (you can get these at any computer-type store) for about $20. Graduate to a higher quality one when you start to do interview products or have some money coming in. Plug it into your computer, and this part is done.

2. Load some free software for podcasts, which you can use to help you promote, tease, and place on your blog. You need two pieces of software that you download and install. (1) Audacity is a free sound editing application (go to www.audacity.sourceforge.net). Select download, open, and it will install. On that same page, you will notice an optional download selection—you need this next. (2) LAME mp3.dll—this is an encoder to save what you say to an MP3 file. This is a necessary step, as the MP3 file is required for universal listening. It will take you to a website called http://lame.buanzo.com.ar. Select the file for your operating system, download and install. It comes in .zip format; double-click to unzip it. Remember where you put the lame mp3.dll file, because you will need it the first time you try to export to MP3.

3. Record what you want to say. We can't cover all of the features here, but once Audacity is installed and loaded, you just click the round, red record button to start recording into your microphone. Hit Stop when completed (the square box). This is where the LAME comes

in. To save your recording as an MP3, click File > Export as MP3. For the first use, it will tell you that you need to locate the LAME file. Refer back to where the file was, and connect it. Future uses will not require this step.

4. Create your podcast file. To record a marketing message or provide a teaser, you can take your MP3 one step further. You can set up your website to allow for a play of the MP3, but what makes a podcast is an RSS file (really simple syndication). This is advanced, and difficult to explain, so for this go to YouTube, and type in "creating a podcast" and you'll see how to do this.

5. Promote your podcast. This is beyond the creation of your product, which was completed at the MP3 stage, but with a podcast—think marketing materials. Sell with your voice, by educating potential buyers and then providing your website link in little infomercials. You can now submit to many podcast directories, especially www.podcastalley.com and the iTunes podcast directory.

Creating a Course/eCourse

If you have an extensive body of knowledge you have been building on a topic that can be taught to someone else, that helps people solve a problem, make money, or achieve a goal, then this may be the product type for you. Again, it is easy to make. You simply speak your knowledge into a microphone, record and convert to an MP3 audio, and then send that to get transcribed and created into a text format, and voilà, you have an eCourse. You can then choose to make this purely a digital download, or something that you ship as CD-ROM and manuals. This will most likely be determined by the price you want to charge.

If you can create an ebook, workbook, and/or audio, then the course/eCourse route is an option that allows you to combine the power of learn and apply, and create a bundled solution that you can sell for a decent price. For this you will need a lot of information that can be learned, followed, and duplicated to produce the promised results. The difference between the course and an eCourse is the delivery method. A course is usually something physical such as binders or CDs, and is shipped as one unit. An eCourse may contain the same materials but is sent electronically either as a download, or over time in a lesson-type format. The advantage to an eCourse is no overhead and delivery issues. The pros to the course is that people get something physical, it is easier to read, and more portable to listen to. The cons of the eCourse is return rates could be higher than a course, and the cons for the course are distribution, delivery, and hard copy costs now have to be considered into the price. Therefore, the price is often less for the eCourse than the course option.

Either digital or hard copy is great, and a product like this is an easy transition to add the next level of the marketing funnel, which could involve a live seminar, coaching, and/or mentoring. If you have a ton of information or interviews, then this opens the door for great continuity product options as well. Get a graphic box, CD, and manual created, and you have yourself a product.

Creating a Continuity Program/Membership Site

This is my favorite and one of my training specialties. It is far too big to cover in this book; I could write a *full* book just on this subject alone. It is slightly more complex than an ebook, but easier than a book and can reap huge rewards. Instead of selling something all in one shot, you can break it up into pieces, call it a "club," and deliver in chunks for a monthly recurring fee. This is continuous revenue, and allows you to start each and every month knowing what you have made already. Predictable, stable income, on automatic, every month. An example I have is www .InternetSuccessMastery.com.

Eight Steps to Creating a Membership Site

1. Decide on a type of membership site you want—for example, monthly, fixed term, buy full access now (I have a monthly site).

2. Decide on the platform (membership software)—for example, WP Wish List, DAP, simple password protect, Amember (I use DAP, digital access pass).

3. Decide on the hook for the membership site. Find yours—for example, work-at-home mom earns six figures, becomes a best-selling author, and international speaker and makes six figures in her *first* six months.

4. Decide on a content delivery schedule—for example, daily, weekly, monthly (I teach weekly, but I run daily, but only after I had 52 weeks of content).

5. Decide on how you will market it—for example, free trial, $1 trial, free gift (I use all of the above).

6. Create the first month of content (arrange in four separate lessons for weekly).

7. Market the membership. This is described in the traffic section.

8. Break it apart to reuse the content—for example, ebook, workbook, stand-alone modules, light version, advanced version with mastermind calls (I do all of the above).

Creating Seminars and Workshops

You can conduct seminars and educate on a one-to-many fashion, or do workshops, where people learn hands-on with something they can duplicate. This is one of my most successful tools. This is a topic so big that I attended a 5-day, 12-hour-a-day training program to learn how to do it well. So I can't cover it all here. If you have attended a pile of events, and think you can do it—go for it. I've done more than 65 of my own events, they always work out, and the cost is relatively cheap.

Five Simple Steps to Creating a Seminar or Workshop

1. Secure a date and location (hotel, boardroom).

2. Decide on duration. Easy is one day or evening.

3. Invite people to it, either via social media, direct e-mail, buy a list, and mail in the local area, send out flyers. This is old-school tactics but it works.

4. You can charge for it, make it nominal and offer to refund when they attend, or make it free and upsell. I have done all three—my favorite is to charge a nominal fee, return it to ensure they come—then make an offer at the event for continuing education.

5. Follow up and make the offer to everyone later.

On Being a Mentor/Coach

If you are doing coaching/mentor programs, there are two requirements you should carefully examine. One, you have done it before and have the knowledge and patience to work one-on-one or one-on-many with varying types of abilities (or know you can do it), and two, you can deliver what you promise. As an added bonus to accelerate your results, have testimonials ready and be able to effectively say why people should pick you.

This is an honorable profession and can be a wonderfully lucrative one, but if you're going to be a mentor or coach then there are certain characteristics that you should evaluate. I am a mentor/coach, and I have mentors/coaches. Take a look and see where you are.

You need to:

- **Be extremely confident and have a good self-image.** When people spend a lot of money with you they are going to expect a lot. You have to be confident enough to maintain what you know and don't let them shake you from it. In addition, continue to get the training required to stay confident and ahead of your clients.

- **Be extremely organized.** You are going to be juggling not only your schedule but other people's as well, so you will need to be able to reference and know all of what they need when they contact you. You may need a software product to help you with this. I use an online system: www.BigContacts.com.

- **Exercise good ethics.** If you are teaching and being a mentor you had better not have any skeletons in the closet, and are keeping your ethics and integrity very high. If people are paying for what you know, they need to be certain that your behavior is worthy of their associating with you.

- **Be highly responsible.** When you help other people you are also assuming a greater sphere of influence, and need to be able to control and assume a level of responsibility for more than yourself.

- **Be clear in your communication.** You are going to be listening and talking to people from many different levels. Some will be newbies, some intermediate, and others will be advanced. Your language has to be such that they understand it based on the prior exposure they may have had in the industry. Clearly state what your offer is, your guarantee, what expectations you have, and what people can expect.

- **Have a broad skill range in your niche.** Clients will come in at varying stages of development, so you will need to have the knowledge across all the levels and be able to teach it, sometimes even when it's not part of the program.

- **Have successfully done what you are coaching/ mentoring.** If you are teaching something make sure that it works and isn't just theoretical. You should have done it yourself, and been able to have someone else do it before you become a mentor or coach and teach it. Not only that, but you need to be successful at it. This ties in a bit that you have the knowledge, you've done it, and others have done it, but goes one step farther in that you are building and expanding on whatever you promise it does, whether that be wealth, health, or anything else.

- **Be enthusiastic and passionate.** You need to be a high-energy, cheerleading, motivational type of person to keep up the energy of both yourself and your client.

- **Be a hard worker.** Being a coach/mentor may be very rewarding, but you have to be a hard worker for this type of product and have the time to run a company and support your clients.

- **Care.** You need to want people to succeed, be happy, get what they came for, and much more, because you feel it is your mission to help people do it. You need to care about people and yourself. Coaching/mentoring isn't just about money; it's about the message you feel compelled to share. Now I'm not saying the money can't be there—to charge what you are worth—what I am saying is don't let money be the motivator.

The other thing you may want to do is to take a look at your role models, mentors, and coaches, and whatever it is you like about them, bring it into your teaching style, too.

Once you have established that this is the revenue avenue for you then you'll need to get some basics in place, and determine how you will run your business.

Three Things You'll Need to Think About When Setting Up Your Mentor/Coaching Product

1. **Delivery method.** Decide how you are going to be mentoring them. Meet for a weekend workshop—then phone and/or e-mail support. One-day workshop—then phone and e-mail. Weekly phone calls and e-mail—one-on-one. Teleseminars—you to many—meet weekly, and so on.

2. **Contact methods.** Are they able to call, phone, or e-mail you? Decide which you will accommodate.

3. **Business structure.** Are you going to operate as a sole proprietor or incorporate? Research the best way for you, and any costs associated.

Four Other Considerations

1. **Payment plans.** Will you expect full payment upfront, over time, three installments, and so on, and will you accept check, credit card, and/or PayPal methods?

2. **Mentor materials.** Will you be providing them with a workbook, eCourse, additional materials, e-mail, PDFs, shipping of materials, videos, and so on?

3. **Scheduling system.** You will need to examine what you are going to use to organize the clients, schedule them, place notes, and so on. The two most common offline methods are ACT! and Goldmine software products or you can use Outlook Contacts. An online method is www.BigContacts.com. You'll also need to handle the communication with them on a one-to-many scale—this can be your autoresponder system—simply set up a category just for them.

4. **Finances building.** A coaching and mentoring practice takes time, as you will need to wear the many hats of a business owner, as well as a coach. As you grow make sure that you are also putting some reserves aside for a rainy day, promotions, and marketing.

Being a coach and building a practice can be difficult. You could experience unforeseen challenges that will test your commitment and decision to continue at times. This is where your passion will need to keep you going. Sometimes your struggles will have to be put aside, as you deal with your clients' needs and wants ahead of your own. You will need to confront many things, keep your integrity high, and know that what you are doing is important, needs to be done, and you feel it is your responsibility to do it.

Once you decide it is the route for you, it is very rewarding. It's like getting paid to help others.

Webinars and Teleseminars

This is something I love to do, and is easy. You can educate and sell a product or service at the end for yourself, or someone else. This is talked about in a future section, but this one is so easy, and you can create a product from it, build a relationship with visitors, give it away for free, or sell on it. I have a full ebook on it with all the steps you can have for free—just go to: www .TeleseminarTradeSecrets.com.

On Being a Speaker

This was a joyous windfall from the book and my coaching. I became a speaker, and even better, an international speaker where my first speaking gig was when I won New Internet Marketing Success of the Year and was flown all expenses paid to speak in front of 3,400 people. Now that's a speaking start. There are three types of speakers: (1) professional, such as National Security Agency (NSA) speakers, get paid to speak; (2) platform, when you get paid based on your sales from the stage (this is what I do); (3) public, when you speak on your topic for free. Whichever route you pick, a whole book and much training go into this skill. I have spent the most money in this field, and it is one of my largest income sources. Sample: www .TracyRepchukLive.com.

Again, I could write a full book on the accolades and steps in being a speaker and getting booked, but for now just know this is an option, and a great one. You can make more in 90 minutes than most people do in a full year selling from the stage.

On Providing a Service

You can simply charge an hourly rate or for a block of time, and use the landing page to capture contact information, and sales page to sell visitors on why they should pick you, right now. If they don't buy right away, you have the contact information to keep working them with your autoresponders.

My very first sale on the Internet was $5,497, Day 2 on the Internet, for selling copywriting services to create a landing page. I posted a page, with a PayPal button, and someone bought (and I never thought it was going to work but I did it anyway). I don't offer this service anymore—it was lucrative but also time-consuming.

To make fast money start with an immediate skill you have like I did, but watch getting stuck in the time-for-money model. If you are selling by the hour, stop it and create a bulk purchase option. It takes the same effort to close, and creates a more consistent revenue stream.

If you have a tangible product such as something you make, have a store front, restaurant, health and beauty products, and so on, the key here will be to have a stable system in place to be able to process orders fast and efficiently. Your landing page and sales page will be working for you, and your time will be spent getting the product out and generating leads. If possible, work toward a digital product that would fit with your product to simplify and expand without extra effort, for example, membership on how to apply makeup.

Network Marketing

If you are in a network marketing endeavor, all the same principles apply. *Always* remember, even if your network marketing provides a landing page and sales page, to collect in your *own* landing page first. That way the list is *yours*. If you send visitors to the offer first, the list is theirs if you leave. The one I am involved with is www.SendGreetingCardsEasily.com (Send Out Cards).

Selling a Tangible Product

Regardless of which product type you select to start your business, you will want to research similar products in that field or niche. You want to see:

- Which ones did really well, and why?

- What will the difference of your product be to those—in other words, your unique selling proposition?

- What are you giving visitors that they couldn't already have gotten from someone else?

- What is the value of the bonuses given by similar products?

- What is the price point of similar products versus what you want yours to be?

- What sales strategy are other marketers using? Examine their sales page and autoresponder cycle. Did you feel inclined to buy? If so, use that information; if not, avoid it.

- If you have a product that is so unique that you can't find any similar products to compare it to, then I hope you did your survey or market research to make sure that it was a needed and wanted product, and you have a target market ready and willing to buy it. Educating a new audience can be expensive.

Methods to research for similar products are the same as when you were researching your niche, only by now you should know who the people are in your industry or niche with the same or similar products, and figure out how you can joint venture with them or create relationships. If your offering is up to their standards, chances are with the right percentage split, and added value opportunity, they may just go for it. (See Joint Venture Basics in Chapter 6 before doing this.) If you don't know them specifically, it will come down to a Google or Yahoo search, entering the keywords you are targeting, and seeing who comes up for the keywords. Check the page one occurrences of each keyword, and start investigating, comparing, and making relationships.

Day 18—Sales Page Creation

The key for you to remember is to select *one* product to start with. Take that *one* product *all* the way from landing page to product creation to sales page to making money. *Do not* try to get them all going at once. You want to get one going, and duplicate the entire sequence and page layouts for the next. Get making money, *then* repeat the formula.

With your product ready to be sold, you now need to create a sales page, to sell for you 24 hours a day, 7 days a week, 365 days a year. If you recall from earlier, the deadly website combo that catapults your sales is landing page to a sales page.

Whereas the autoresponders (e-mail) are your sales team and gets chunk-size benefits continuously educating visitors, this is the first point of contact after the landing page, and your best shot at closing them *now*. This is where the integration of your story and your ability to do direct sales copywriting will come in handy. This is the piece that will close them on the spot.

In the sales page debate, there is constant talk about short versus long. For now, it is still long (but not 42-page crazy long, more like an organized 7-page long). However, you still have to use your subheadlines and your bottom line offer in a stand-alone way to sell the scanners (the type who rush straight down to the bottom of the page to see the price). The key to success here is to follow what works, follow the money, and do what studies indicate.

Top Sales Page Tips

- **One purpose.** This one-page site is designed to highlight the benefits of one product or service. It is a direct campaign to focus visitors to do one thing: buy your product. That is why in this type of site, ask them to buy 11 to 15 times at various peak points, until they finally get the message. Like the landing page, this page has a specific design, layout, and art to it. Near misses can be inches away from soaring sales. It combines headline, subdeck, purchaser benefits, history, testimonials, keywords, a story, rapport, lead, credibility, value justification, risk reversal, bonuses, and continues along this line until it either closes the sale, or they leave. The great thing is if you have captured their name via the landing page—that is okay if they leave—now you can build a relationship with them via the autoresponder messages, so it isn't lost yet.

- **Headline.** Size 5 text, bold, and grabs their attention. This is the first thing visitors see. You use your headline to draw them in like a black widow. You have only seconds to keep them reading. This skill is also heavily used in the subheads, which are the headlines/titles that appear throughout the copy that assist in carrying the story, breaking up the text to keep it manageable, and allowing the scanner type of people to read just those and still be sold when they see the price.

- **Copywriting/rapport.** Direct your text to your target audience as tightly as you can. Address the language and emotional tone of that audience in a way that you would talk to them, and remember to tell them constantly what is in it for them. The copywriting is critical because it needs to continue to captivate the readers until they are sold, and do this in the few minutes they are willing to donate to you. You must also integrate keywords that are critical to your being discovered by search queries. And last but not least, you need to have your story weave through all of it, keeping them captivated and attached and relating to you.

- **Testimonials.** Have your testimonials in a pale-color box, with full name and picture if possible. If you can, have an audio or video supplement.

- **Personalization** (who is the sales page from). Your name, location, date, and time appear to give the sales page the appearance of being just posted and updated regularly. Add the subject and address them and you're ready to go.

- **Tagline.** Use your unique selling proposition (USP) to tell visitors why you or your products are special and why they should buy this item. Have your tagline and use it often. Establish what yours is and work it, along with your story.

- **Text and highlighting.** The text is often done in Verdana or Arial, and is varied using size, bold, yellow highlights, font color basic is black, but varies with critical text or headlines done in red, blue, or maroon.

- **Bonus gifts.** This is a classic component, and is the closing part of the pitch. You give visitors so many extras that the offer is irresistible, and they purchase your product. The bonus is on average 10 times the value of the actual item.

- **Call to action.** The call to action is what you want visitors to do. Buy now, buy now, buy now. Make it a time-, space-, or quantity-limited offer to increase urgency and expedite the purchase.

- **Links.** There are no links that take visitors out of that one page. You can have order links, contact links, about links, support links, but that will take them somewhere within the one page. Only use pop-ups or links within the page to direct the flow, or offer another option on leaving.

- **Video and audio.** This is a nice addition and can increase the conversion rate by being able to inform people faster with less effort on their part. Audio is a great way to direct them exactly on what you want them to do, and video is good for testimonials and demonstrations of proof. This adds to the experience while they are reading the site. You can control more when you add audio/video, and in some cases close the sale without doing anything else.

The sales page website is a complete course in itself, and if you don't have experience in this area I recommend either hiring someone for your first one, or studying sites that contain all of the sales page elements successfully, and duplicate the format. Study layout and copywriting with story integration. I imagine hiring for a sales page is a hefty investment even on the bidding sites. If you're going to try elance.com or guru.com to quote on your job, make sure the person has direct sales page experience and check it out thoroughly. A solid investment in copywriting will be money well spent (I have had three mentors for a total of $23,500 in just this topic). When I started, it was one of my earliest investments right after how to create the landing page. Copywriting is the skill that is required to sell.

Lastly, you really want to spend time checking out the sales pages of others in your niche, and pull out the best features of those and incorporate them into your own. Search your competitors and find out what their sales page sites look like, and if you are in an industry where they aren't using them, then you have just walked into a mecca money-making opportunity because you'll be closing sales faster than anyone else ever imagined possible.

For a sample sales page, one of my clients built this herself from the instructions in one of my courses. You can go to www.howtoachieveyourgoals.com.

Pricing Your Product

Pricing your product is an important step, especially when you are designing various products for various stages of your market funnel. Every error could mean lost sales or money left on the table.

There are two ways to estimate price:

1. **Industry average.** Look at what your competition is selling at or use an industry average. Consider this a starting point and compare how your product stacks up. I would recommend this method combined with split-testing.

2. **Split-testing.** This is where you set one offer up at the competition's or industry-suggested price, and also set one up that is lower, and one that is higher. You launch the first one to a sample on your list; launch the second to another sample, and a third to the final sample. From this you will be able to see how many people checked out the offer versus how many bought the offer, and what that produced gross sales–wise. Whichever performed the best in this test period is what you select for your entire database.

For example:

	Lower Price	Industry Average	Higher Price
Sell price	$197	$297	$497
Number who checked it out	100	100	100
Number who bought	37	23	17
Gross profit	$7,289	$6,831	$8,449

From this example you can see the higher price pulled in the best results, with the least volume, but you don't know that unless you test. Once you have gotten this you could actually test again because you have a unique database of subscribers and it is best to learn your optimum price from them. You could test between $497 and $597 to see once again what price came out on top gross profit-wise.

It may reveal that your lowest price is the best with high-quantity purchases, or the industry average prevailed. This is a statistically correct way to set your price, and will get you the optimum price and prevent you from leaving money on the table.

The Irresistible Offer

Bonus products, aka *the irresistible offers*, were first coined by Mark Joyner, and are a standard technique in Internet marketing. Offers have become so intricate that the bonus is many times more in value than the actual product being purchased. This is why it is called *irresistible*—you are putting together an accumulation of benefits and products that are so powerful that visitors buy. This is a major benefit for the purchaser and even better is that the offers rarely cost anything to get.

There are few industries that deliver as beautifully as the Internet marketers do. We give, and give, and give, and sure we can say that it does not cost visitors anything extra—but these "bonus offers" can be the make or break point in a deal. They are a successful strategy in the sale and promotion of your product and you need to have them if you want to play the Internet game.

Bonus products consist of audios, teleseminar recordings, interviews, ebooks, software, and your time. Do you want to know how to get products for your bonus offers?

> **BONUS OFFER TIP**
>
> If you are worried you won't be able to find any bonus gifts to offer with your product, it is simple, and the answer will surprise you—*just ask!*

I asked for a bonus product to include people I could find who were appropriate to my industry, and they all said yes. It is free promotion and goodwill for them, and once they're established they often have products they can afford to do this with. It is a great way to attract more new traffic and possible affiliates. Win-win again.

If you see a free bonus offer provided by someone on another website, search google.com for JV giveaways—JV = joint venture—and giveaways are sites where people give their products away in exchange for a subscriber. You can check these out. If you see a product that would fit your needs, ask the owners of the giveaway product by opting-in to their list. They'll probably give it to you. You just have to let them know what you will be doing with it, and the product it will be affiliated with. Once they know this is similar or beneficial, they will more than likely agree.

The other ways to get bonus offer products is to purchase resell and master resell rights (check to make sure, though, that you are allowed to give away; some specify you have to sell them). Resell rights allow you to sell; master resell rights allow you to sell the rights to sell the whole package. More value can be placed on these at bonus time, that is, $197 versus $497.

A great site for inexpensive resell and master resell rights products is www.master-resale-rights.com.

Each product should have many bonus offers, almost at 10 times the value of the product. (See Figure 4.2.) Your offer

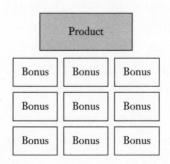

Figure 4.2   Product Offer with Bonuses Structure

can make or break the sales and can even be the cause of it (not to devalue your product, but it is good to get the sale any way you can).

The Truth about Testimonials

When you are first starting out it can be difficult to get testimonials, but the truth is, you need them. You may have to give your product to a friend, or have someone test it out for you. You need to do this anyway to make sure it works and can be duplicated without your being involved (in the software industry we call this beta testing). Your friends will be able to troubleshoot your cycle, show you where it got confusing, or if there were missing steps. Once the product is tested, I'm sure they'll gladly give you a testimonial.

A testimonial is used on your sales page, your landing page, your YouTube channel. Anywhere you promote your product or service, you should have a testimonial. This is your social proof. There are five things to consider when getting testimonials:

1. Use a full name, city, and state, and if applicable the person's company name, product, or website link. The person needs to be real. A couple of initials doesn't mean anything and looks like you are making it up. If the people used the product and it worked, they will want the back link for their own self-promotion, and you need the information as proof.

2. If you can, also get a picture of the people. Readers get more reality when they can see something.

3. If you want to take it up a notch, record the testimonial using a teleseminar service, or direct from your phone to your PC.

4. If you are doing workshops, seminars, or coaching, and you are with the people at some point, take a webcam and set up your PC to record them for your website. Have them go to a "Testimonial Station," set them up, and let them go at it. If you do this directly after a successful event the testimonials will last you for years. The alternative is to have a camcorder and get it recorded and converted. Although I have found when they do it alone at a station, they are far more relaxed.

5. Use them. Sounds simple, but once you have collected your testimonials use them anywhere you can. They aren't to be brought out only on special occasions like Mom's fine China; they are yours to exploit and be proud of. Get them all on YouTube as well and promote them anywhere.

The truth about testimonials is to be sure to get a testimonial any way you can especially when you are starting out. Build from there, looking, asking, and seeking for every opportunity you can to grab another. Nothing gives more confidence to a prospect than somebody else promoting you. This is necessary social proof.

Protecting Your Assets

Protecting yourself and your assets as you are building often gets overlooked in the search for your dreams. There is a tendency to put up a website, make a promise, sell something, and wait. Make sure that your websites and you are protected, which is critical. Once you get a website up, it is a good idea to get the legal requirements of your websites in compliance. If you are at the point where you have a website (or many) and are promoting your own products, or affiliate products, there are certain things you need to know in order to ensure that you are safe, your assets are protected, and you adhere to web legislations with respect to things such as privacy laws. I'm not a lawyer so I don't want to get specific about this, but I want to make sure that you investigate protection as part of your business plan.

I would recommend that you take a look at www .WebLawCompliance.com, which was created by attorneys to bulletproof your websites. You need to understand the legal requirements of doing business online and use forms provided to get in compliance for this, and the CAN-SPAM Act. Just one mistake will cost you far more and for this price, the peace of mind is well worth it. In addition, when you are setting up your sites, go to this site and learn how to properly set up site maps and become compliant by Google standards.

Visitors want a site map. Here's a good site: www.Google .com/webmasters/sitemaps.

Day 19—Affiliate Program: You Selling for Others

An affiliate program where you sell for others is a way to possibly make some fast, easy cash. No product, no shipping, all you have to do is send people to the offer and hope they buy. However, you need either a list to market to, or you need to know how to get traffic or use Google AdWords to send traffic to the offer. This leads us back to "the power is in the list." This is called a *pay-for-performance* model and is like a modern-day "finders' fee" where individuals who introduce new clients to a business are compensated. In this model the advertiser only pays if a new client results in a sale or a lead, which creates a low-risk, high-reward plan for both parties. The compensation rates can vary but usually range from 35 percent to 50 percent, with a possible second tier, which rewards you a percentage for the sales the person you signed up made as well. The ultimate program has a recurring option where you are paid monthly a percentage of what the purchaser pays. This occurs in membership-based products.

The Benefits of an Affiliate Program

- **It's passive income.** You don't have to work hard at it.

- **You *do not* need to have a product.** If you are just looking for some extra income streams, all you have to do is send prospects to the offer and collect checks.

- **You *do not* need a website.** You don't have to get a domain, host it, make a site, worry about HTML, worry about copywriting, it's all written and done for you.

- **Unlimited.** You can join as many affiliate programs as you want.

- **Worry-free.** You don't need to worry about anything such as product shipping, delivery, customer-relationship building, it is all done for you. Always remember though, don't send an affiliate lead to a program *until* you have captured them in your own database first. This will take a landing page and autoresponder system, but it is crucial for long-term benefits and big payoffs. Commission checks are nice but the big bucks are in the list. Once you get a list you simply offer your subscribers details about the next affiliate program, and take advantage of a new revenue stream instantly, without a full campaign or rebuild. The ultimate program has a recurring option where you are paid monthly a percentage of what the purchaser pays. This occurs in membership-based products.

There's one caveat, though—affiliate money is not a magic potion. Many people will tell you that you can make millions by just selling affiliate products, and it's push button, set and forget, and it is fast cash today. There is a *lot* more to it than that. The piece they forget to tell you is that you need a list or know how to generate traffic—two skills that often come later in your learning. Having said that, though, affiliate programs are a great source of revenue, and I use them in my membership sites and within my autoresponder series.

Three Ways You Can Find Affiliate Programs That Suit You

1. If you have found companies that sell products in the same niche as yours during your niche and product research cycle, then join their affiliate programs. You can then offer them until your product is ready, or in addition to yours.

2. You can do a search in Yahoo! and Google. Enter your (niche) affiliate programs and see what comes up. Check them out, and join if appropriate, for example, dog products affiliate programs.

3. You can go to companies such as www.Clickbank.com or www.cj.com (Commission Junction), www.shareasale .com, www.affiliateprograms.com, or www.linkshare.com

and open up a free account, and search in their enormous database for similar products, and offer those.

Being prepared to be an affiliate:

- If you don't have a list, you will need to set up a Google AdWords campaign to drive traffic to it.

- Google AdWords is an art, so you'll want to learn this technology in order for it to benefit you. You can check out the section in this book about Google AdWords plus go here to learn from the creators, http://google.com/adwords.

- You should have a lead capture system (i.e., landing page and autoresponder) for your own future product (or to create the list as the product). I recommend that instead of sending the lead directly to the offer and losing the prospect forever, direct them instead to your own landing page and capture their information, get them on your list, and then send them to the offer. This is a key to making affiliate programs really pay off for you, especially if you undertook a Google campaign to get them to it.

- Join a few affiliate programs, keep track, watch how they do, drop the ones that don't work, and keep the ones that do. Continue to do this until you have a hefty lineup of strong products that bring in the income and future leads you are looking for.

- Some of the best affiliate products are any that have a recurring factor such as a membership site, so that once you get them in, you get paid as long as they remain a member. So look for these first.

Adding affiliate programs is a great thing to do while your product is being built, or if you just want some passive income. Plus, it helps you get familiar with the market, the possible joint venture partners there are, and how to sell and market effectively without a large investment on your part.

DAY 20—AFFILIATE PROGRAM: OTHERS SELLING FOR YOU

Having other people sell for you is one of the most successful things you can do for your product. An army of supporters helping you sell for no cost, except to provide them with your sales and marketing information, which you already have, is a bargain next to the old-fashioned hire a sales rep way.

The first thing you should do as soon as your product is ready and you have tested your marketing material, sales website, and ads, is put together an affiliate program. Sign up for Clickbank, Commission Junction, iBill, and if you have a product such as 1shoppingcart, get it integrated so you can track the sales of your resellers and pay them promptly.

Top Five Reasons Why You Should Have an Affiliate Program

1. **Free sales team.** Affiliates are one of the cheapest and easiest ways to roll out a successful product quickly. Purchasing millions of e-mail, banner, or website impressions is expensive and risky. Once you have a successful product, opening up an affiliate program is the fastest way to get free exposure to millions of potential customers.

2. **Cost-effective use of your time.** You have to create a campaign for yourself; why not have that effort applied across thousands versus just you and bring in an exponential amount of money.

3. **Long-term product shelf-life.** When you launch a program a great deal of effort goes into it, but after you get your initial payoff, you move to your next one. While you're busy creating your next product, this one is still being sold by your trusty team.

4. **More is better.** You can't conquer the Internet yourself, and the more relationships you establish, the farther your reach will be. This will result in more sales, joint venture relationships, links, and more people who know and like you.

5. **Customer relationship building.** You have this as part of your sales cycle, but it is even more powerful when it's part of your affiliate cycle. It builds a legion of loyal supporters who will become loyal customers. They have agreed to represent you, and most good affiliates sell what they believe in.

Once you have your program together, make sure you treat your affiliates well.

- Thank them for being a part of your team. Send personalized e-mail, videos, and give them tips, features, tricks, and updates about your product. Send them new testimonials, anything that keeps them connected and helps them sell more.

- Make it easy for them to sell for you. Give them their link or replicated site, all the e-mail campaigns, text boxes, banners, whatever you have, in an easy format they can scoop and use.

- Give them a better than average rate. If you want to see what really helps people sell your product, just give them a great split and they will go the extra mile. Give them a second tier as well. Nothing will motivate affiliates more than the money they get.

- Think of every affiliate sale as gravy. Think of it as a sale you wouldn't have otherwise gotten; that way when you are paying out your affiliate fees, it won't bother you at all. Focus on the piece you keep, not the piece you are giving.

- Share the wealth. The most successful Internet marketers share the wealth, so if you want to "Follow the guy with the biggest pile of cash, and do what they do"—this means to do it the way they do. Join their program, and use it as a guideline in the creation of your own program.

Affiliate programs, whether you are selling for someone else or using them to sell your products, are a great way to add multiple income streams to your strategy, and expand your network of connections. In general, I recommend doing all three: being an affiliate, getting your own affiliate network set up once you have your own product, and creating the list as a product. One day very soon, you'll see why. To start your affiliate program, be sure to check out:

www.Clickbank.com

www.cj.com (Commission Junction)

www.shareasale.com

www.linkshare.com

Using Video and Audio to Promote

Video and audio are an integral part of your marketing, and are no longer a luxury. You need people to get familiar with you fast, and video is the best way to do that. You don't need it to be fancy and professional, but you need to have a video with one purpose, one message, and make that message clear.

It also isn't difficult any more. Buy a flip camera and you can make a video, upload it to YouTube, and pull into your page in less than 30 minutes for your first time, and five minutes once you get familiar with doing it.

The only debate left is whether you play it automatically when they arrive, or have them initiate the audio by selecting play. That decision is up to you—but conversions are higher if it automatically plays; however, you can also alienate some people who will leave because it alarmed them or they were in a place where audio wasn't appropriate. I prefer they hit play themselves.

Video can improve opt-in and sales rates by up to 80 percent. I like it, I use it, and I recommend it to my clients.

Top 12 Reasons Why Having Video on Your Site Works

1. Gets their attention fast.

2. Holds their attention with the extrasensory appeal.

3. Controls the flow of the information, where they look, when they react, and what they are supposed to do.

4. Lets you really drill in the features while they are looking around, or glancing at other things. You can get the data in fast.

5. Lets you express the benefits in a way that they will understand as they are listening and viewing.

6. It adds value to the experience.

7. You can add your story similar to the autoresponder cycle, but in one quick action that increases the speed at which they react and buy.

8. You can add a comprehension to the cycle that brings all of your components together, increasing awareness and understanding.

9. You can elicit and convey emotion more effectively.

10. You can inspire, motivate, and build confidence and a connection to you.

11. You can have fun, and add it to your websites, your blog, anything you do, either informally or formally.

12. You can push visitors to a call to action, and make sure they do what you want them to do by keeping them focused, and then directing them until the goal is achieved.

Audio and video are effective tools and with your passion and sense of fun, you can give them a 30-second pitch they'll never forget and dramatically improve the results you are looking for. There are lots of available technologies ranging from free on upward. It will depend on your technical ability and which choice works best for you.

Recommended sites are www.thebestvideogear.com and www.Amazon.com.

Once you have video, check out Chapter 6's YouTube and Video Sites section to see what you can also do with it, in addition to putting it on your site.

Remember to also get this on your blog once you've created it. Images and video increase the page value of your blog in the eyes of Google.

CHAPTER 4 ACTION PLAN

- Select your product type.
- Research similar products.
- Create your product.
- Put together the sales site.
- Find your bonus offers.
- Join an affiliate program.
- Set up an affiliate program if applicable.

CHAPTER 5

Tapping into Marketing Miracle Makers

Why You Should Consider a Mentor

In the world of Internet marketing, we are often individually holed up in our homes or offices, mining the Internet for opportunities and creating our empires.

There are many ways you can become successful on the Internet, but most are the hard way, the costly way, the long way, or the mentor way. The hard way is to do it yourself. The costly way is to do it yourself. The long way is to do it yourself. Then, there is the mentor way. You will hear stories of the pioneers of the industry and how they made it, but they will no doubt tell you that it was hard, costly, and long. These are people who we need to be grateful for and to ask for help. No matter who I meet, from guru to newbie, they thank some mentor for getting them where they are, or started. I have had more than 24 mentors already, and will continue to invest until there is no higher I can reach (which really means forever). There is a big barrier that prevents many people from achieving their ultimate Internet dreams and I call it the big fat lie.

TIP

A common thread of success stories is people got help either through a partner or mentor. You have to do it yourself, but you don't have to do it alone.

Now I'm not saying you *can't* do it all by yourself, but you will discover that it is a lonely and difficult way to get to success. If you can't trust other people, how do you expect others to trust you? If you can't ask for help, how can you expect others to want help from you?

You need to approach Internet marketing keeping four things in mind:

1. Knowing where you are—and *why*.

2. Knowing where you are going—and *why*.

3. Knowing the best way to get there.

4. Getting there quickly and easily.

This is an industry where the data and information change so quickly that taking on all of that by yourself will prove to be overwhelming, exhausting, and really frustrating. I don't wish that on anyone. This market is a millionaire maker's dream, and that is why so many chase it. Many, however, approach it with pessimism, dabble here and there, make a few inquiries, check some stuff out. Others may spend a fortune on reference and course materials but never find themselves standing at the top of the mountain. If this is what you have experienced, then you need to get a mentor. The pace of the industry dictates that getting direct help from a person helps to improve your success exponentially.

Having a mentor is the inside track to model a successful person. Why do you think shows such as *The Apprentice* are so enticing? It's not just the media exposure, but for the winner it's a chance to work closely with a billionaire such as Donald Trump. Guess what that would do for your learning curve and mind-set? You would be influenced by a person who has mastered his or her art.

For anyone considering getting a mentor, even though the cost may seem high, if you choose based on the mentor analysis you will more than likely not only get your money's worth, you will get someone you can depend on to get you to the top faster, easier, and in the long run, cheaper.

Day 21—Mentor Analysis

This was my favorite part of putting the book together because it was a combined test of what I did to select my mentors, and then after contacting almost every expert out there for an interview, how they responded. Now I know these guys are crazy busy and many don't do interviews, but in general, I was pleased at the courteousness of many, and the stellar performance of some.

When you are joining a mentor or coaching program, it can range from about $2,500 to $15,000 depending on the access and time frame. I do recommend that you pick at least one mentor because if you want to be a part of the game, you need to move from the bench to the field fast. Here are 13 things you need to consider in your mentor analysis:

1. **Who will you be working with?** If it isn't directly with the expert in some capacity, whether it is a review cycle, or the training and coaching, or teleseminars— then I would think twice. If you are getting someone who was coached by them, it isn't the same. I made a $5,000 error here by getting someone who was coached, but not the one. He could do it for himself but had no idea how to teach others how to make it work. They are two very different skills.

2. **Do they have access via teleseminar/e-mail/club?** As part of the program, is there a club element where you continue to get access to teleseminars or other members, and is there a way to ask questions and get answers? Is there a period of private e-mail or phone access to keep the program moving? A question you can ask is: "After our initial time, what happens next?"

3. **Do they have support staff?** When you have purchased an eCourse or mentoring, if mentors have someone that can help you as well, this is a big plus. If the package includes web hosting, software, or technical help, this is an important factor. Lastly, find out how hard it is to get access to your mentor when the time isn't scheduled—whether it be e-mail or social media.

4. **What extras do they provide?** I have received everything from free web hosting for the year, to a laptop with everything preloaded, to simply what you bought—which in some cases was a program that was just a website with ebooks on it, and two more new ones a month. Be sure to know exactly what you are getting for your money, with your main focus on getting access and time with the mentor.

5. **What is their specialty?** The Internet is an enormous field and even the category Internet marketing encompasses a vast range of skills. Each mentor has something he or she excels at. For some it's marketing/promotion, some it's joint ventures, books, millionaire makers, traffic, corporate strategists, and the list goes on. You need to determine your niche, your core, and then select your first mentor based on where you are,

and what he or she provides. *This is the most costly mistake right here*—buying beyond where you are, for a niche you are not involved with.

6. **What is their guarantee?** Do not go into a mentor program looking at the guarantee, and thinking you have that time frame to get your money back. That is a surefire way of not achieving what you want, except maybe your money back, and a year gone by.

   You can find out what it is to appease your element of fear of spending the money, but then throw it away and do not think about it. Because if you work toward your goal as if you have to make it, even if to just recoup your investment, the results will be much greater. Then at the end of the time period you will not need to worry about the guarantee because you will not need it.

7. **Focus on the time access to the mentor.** The golden nugget of a mentor program is the actual time you will get to speak with or be taught or supported by the mentor. Do not get swayed by all of those pages of lovely bonuses. They are fantastic, and great, but the differentiating factor to compare programs is the "time with the coach." Is it a weekend, almost 20 hours of time, plus calls afterward? Is it one call a month, or a one-hour consult after you have done the program on your own? This is a key, because all of the bonus gifts are gravy, so ignore those completely until you have plucked out that nugget and are comparing apples to apples.

8. **Pick one mentor to start and stay focused.** Once you enter the game of Internet marketing and sign up

for the various ezines to keep on top of what is going on, you will be bombarded with so much information that it is easy to get overwhelmed. Then, confused. Then be driven into a feeling that you know so little that learning it all will be impossible. This is why the goal planning of Chapter 1 is so important.

Look at your goal, and do one thing at a time. This is why putting together a list of what you want to accomplish for that day is a necessity. It is so easy to get moved from tree to tree like a homeless monkey. You need to hold your position in space, keep your focus, know your goal, do one thing at a time, and you will get there.

9. **How long have they been around?** I would examine how long a person has been in the industry, or what experience he or she has in being a coach/mentor from another field. I have been to a few seminars where the new guys who have just broken in are now offering mentoring services. There are pros and cons to this. The pros are the offers they make that are usually out of this world. Tons of prime time with them for a bargain price. Prices you will not see next time.

The possible downside is if their success has been recent, they may need to stabilize their program. This does not mean prove it; they have done that. This means they need to get the business foundation and structure secure before they start pulling in people to support. The build-up to breaking through is intense and then the next year is primarily delivery and growth. During these two Phase I stages they have to get their business model in place and move from the one-man-band I can do it all myself, to a true business entity.

10. **Success stories.** Watch for the inbreeding of success stories. This is where the experts give each other a testimonial. It is great to have the support of a guru for the product and it does speak to its value, but we know the gurus can get stuff to work. You need to look for whether the average Joe off the street with a dream and desire can pull it off. These are the ones I look for.

11. **Personality.** This goes to the fact that you like the people. You want to be with them, you think they are great, you can relate well, and their training style fits your lifestyle. If these are people you are going to trust, put your faith in, and listen to intently, you have to like them or at least respect them.

12. **Price.** Now you may have been looking for this farther up the list, but this is really where it belongs. You have to consider all of the above and then look at this. If you are at the beginning stages of your journey, you will usually discover once you have evaluated all of the above, there are certain mentors you are not ready for, regardless of price. Their focus might be business strategy or wealth building; and you are just starting and need a landing page. It is great to want the guru at the top of the mountain but in the beginning you need access to the person, and learning from just CDs can be overwhelming. So get the mentor for the exact focus you need right now, for the top price you can afford to pay, with the most amount of direct access, with someone you really like—and price will not matter.

13. **Next level.** You will soon discover as you complete a portion of your business or project or product, you

are ready for the next person. You will have many mentors throughout your journey who will serve different purposes for different stages. As you become more experienced, more wealthy, and more in demand, you will need the guidance and structure of people like Jay Abraham, Joel Bauer, Rich Schefren, and Dan Kennedy. You will also discover the mentors you use also use these guys. It is a tiered system of education and graduation, and it is a fun and exciting game to play. Take your baby steps or your giant leaps always with your goal in mind, because the path has already been paved; you just need to walk it.

BUILDING YOUR TEAM

This book is designed so that *you* see where you are in the progression of building an Internet marketing business, and then selecting a mentor who can help you with that step. In my case, I help you with most of the major steps—from niche selection, to website building to traffic methods. I deal end to end, like this book.

However, when you hit some sections, you may want that to be such a major focus that you need to find someone specific for that.

For example, here are a few mentors and some I have used, along with the products they specialize in (and what I do):

- Tracy Repchuk—Done-for-you brand and websites
- Joel Bauer—Event training
- Alex Mandossian—Teleseminars
- James Malinchak—Speaker training
- Ray Edwards and Alan Forrest Smith—Copywriting

The other area I would invest in is specialized traffic methods, social media, YouTube, copywriting, and outsourcing. If you are ready for outsourcing, here is the team I use: www.EasyOutsourcingNow.com.

DAY 22—SELECT A MENTOR

I sum up this section in one sentence: Select a mentor. You can buy a book and get an idea of what you need to do to make your business work, but it is designed for you to follow the steps, and where possible, get a mentor for the step you are at. I have had people tell me that working through my book was the first money they ever made on the Internet. You can get an eCourse or Google AdWords or AdSense working, too—but if you are going to get into this field it is much more fun when you are part of the community, and getting the most you can. This is an industry that has a huge learning curve that requires time and money. If someone is telling you otherwise, I have not seen that work yet. It is what we all want to be true, but the reality is that you have to do what it takes to get what you want. You did not get your current job without any skills or training, and this is no different. If you are reading this and saying "I have already spent a fortune and gotten nowhere except in debt or more confused," then this unfortunately goes back to starting at the beginning first. There are scammers out there, but for a program to work you need your goals, your niche, your focus, a landing page, and so on established. It is not a good strategy to see yet another magic money-making product get released, get it, try it, and if results are not what are expected, go to the next thing. Same goes for selecting a mentor without your core focus, or else how will you know what skills or products are appropriate and fit within your scope? Selecting a mentor based on the next step you need to do will "add to your foundation."

Pick one thing you have right now, for example, an ebook with resell rights, and get that working. Once you can get one thing working, you can get another, and another. If you have a long trail of products that you cannot get to work, more products will not help. You need to have each prior element working before you can keep moving forward, one step at a time.

If you have an ebook, choose this, because you can get three types of products from that (do one at a time, though, that is, sell the book, sell the rights, sell the master resell rights). Take this one concept and take it through the three cycles (and each through the 31-day program), and ignore all the fancy and hyped-up offers that will come across your desk as the next best moneymaker, faster, easier, and with little or no cost. *Stay focused*. The rest is just adding to your confusion. Sometimes you will hear of overnight successes and $1,000,000 payouts in 30 days and these are true stories; however, you are missing the backstory that created those instant sensations. This is not the lottery, although after much hard work it can sure feel like it. If you interview or research the background of the guys at the top, and those in the middle, and those just breaking out from the bottom, they all have a common thread—they got help, and this help costs either time, money, or both. If you choose your mentor properly and complete the program you purchase, the money you spend on mentor after mentor until you have gotten where you want to be will be a drop in the bucket compared to the return you receive.

We address one more issue in this section: your responsibility in all of this. Just because you have your mentor or eCourse or your books, this guarantees only what you are willing to put into it with your time and effort. The only person who can guarantee your success is you. You are the author of your life. You paint the canvas, walk into it, and act out the scene. Now that is a harsh reality if your life is sucking, but it is true—you got yourself where you are today. Having said that, though, this is where the good part comes in. You can also get yourself out and create a better future. Nobody else will do it for you. If you are not creating your future by being at cause, then it is getting painted for you while you operate at effect.

Internet marketing success is about being at cause. Internet marketers cause things to happen, industries to shift, wealth to be created, lives to be improved, and it is available to anyone who reaches for it and is willing to be at cause while he or she navigates it. A mentor can only help in the ratio you are willing to make things happen. Mentors are not a magic pill designed to paint your world and make it all better for you. They are the role models and the people who have created a system that is working, can be duplicated to work for others, has been tested and proven, and can also work for you.

The other common thread you will find with mentors is that they worked very hard to be able to relax. In the typical job situation, you work very hard—period. The end of the rainbow is retirement. That is a long way away for most, and a crappy age to be able to relax, not to mention the lifestyle you may have to adjust to. By the time many people hit that stage they do not feel like relaxing, they have somehow been deemed "no longer worthy of being in the workforce." So expect to work very hard to become an overnight success. With the accelerated knowledge from a mentor, though, and the other materials that are available for your niche, it is not a 60-year struggle, but it might just be a six-month struggle—in the grand scale of time, it is a blip on the radar and a drop in the bucket.

Mentors are role models so select one you like, can relate to, who communicates to you, and puts you at the starting point of where you are. From day one I invested in mentors because as an entrepreneur I know that investing in yourself is the most valuable action you can take. I pick one who is where I want to be for my next level. If you select mentors who are too far beyond your income and skill level, you will not be able to keep up. They will move too fast, think too fast, and expect more than you can give. You also want to make sure they are making things happen in their own life, applying what they learn and not just learning and parroting it back to you. That is easy.

You have much on your plate with your goals, implementing all of the steps, creating a product, meeting people, getting your mentor, selling, marketing, growing, and juggling it, all at the same time.

At some point you will need to build a team around you, and that will include your mentors, joint venture (JV) partners, friends, family, subcontractors, and eventually staff, to handle all of the stuff you do not want to.

You need to invest in mentor programs that will help. Do not just keep buying more products and courses, and trying to figure them out on your own. Invest in an expert who will be your mentor or contact point. You will notice that the major difference between Internet millionaires and everyone else is that those people pulled in a team of experts around them. They got mentors. (When I started I invested in a mentor a month— because each one had a field of expertise, and it was the start of my team.) So start building your team to help you, and then help others to achieve their goals.

You will notice in the Internet world that mentors have mentors have mentors, and it goes on. I mentor and coach people, and I have mentors and coaches, and they have mentors and coaches. Invest in yourself, and think of it as training and education. You probably paid for school at one point—well, this is no different—continuing education in a virtual world. Even with my almost 30-year history as an entrepreneur and computer software developer, I need help all of the time. Technology moves very fast and a team of experts keeps you organized and on track. This can include good contacts you find for web development and copywriting from elance.com or guru.com or getafreelancer.com.

There are tons of choices out there, and I wish you the best with your selections and team.

CHAPTER 5 ACTION PLAN

Choose a mentor based on the analysis and your niche/goals. Start with someone you can afford, and step your way up to the ultimate option. Even if you cannot afford one, pick and follow one.

Chapter 6

Creating Your Traffic Hurricane

C hapters 1 through 5 focused on many of the free traffic and easy-to-implement link strategies, but now that you have your product, it's time to do some serious marketing.

Day 23—PPC, Google AdWords, and Facebook

Pay per click (PPC) is when you create an ad and pay for the ad when somebody sees it, and clicks through to check out the offer. It sounds wonderful—free advertising—but this is an art, and a game that should be entered into carefully.

Google AdWords is the biggest player in the PPC game, but Facebook ads are quickly gaining popularity because of the power to specifically target an exact market. Regardless of which you choose, you need to learn the rules and then follow them. For Facebook you need a Facebook account and then click on the flower-like symbol in the upper right corner and select Create Ad from the drop down box. For Google, your first step is to open up a Google AdWords account. This is free to do; you simply go to http://adwords.google.com/select/Login. This link takes you to a page where you can either log in or create an account if you have not already. (If you have a Google AdWords or blogger account from earlier, you can use the same ID and password.)

Once you are ready to create an ad, you need to think of your ad in terms of four lines. This is where finely crafted, optimized keywords come into play.

> **TIP**
>
> Headline—25 characters
> Benefit or problem solve—35 characters
> Benefit or problem solve—35 characters
> Website link

This is your entire template to attract customers without it costing you a fortune. The design is optimized to the attention span of an Internet user. Your fate lies in how well you master the manipulation of headlines and corresponding sentences to create a pull to your landing page or affiliate product.

When creating your campaign there are two ways you can target for traffic:

1. **Keyword-targeted**—This is the most popular method. AdWords is based on matching relevant ads to a user's web search or browsing experience. Keywords are critical to helping both a user find the information they're looking for, and helping an advertiser reach that user with ads that relate to the user's web experience.

   When you build your ad groups, you'll select keywords to help target your ads for search so they reach people precisely when they're looking for what you have to offer. To do that, you'll need to pick one of the following match types for each keyword:

   • **Broad match** is the default setting for all keywords. All searches made using your keyword (in any order or combination) might display your ad. Searches for similar or related queries might also trigger your ad.

- **Phrase match** narrows your reach by requiring the words to appear in that exact order.

- **Exact match** further narrows your reach by showing your ad when the exact phrase is used in the search — without any other words before, between, or after.

- **Negative match** eliminates searched phrases you don't want your ad to appear for, such as *cheap* or *free*.

- **Embedded match** allows you to prevent your ad from appearing in relation to certain phrase or exact matches.

2. **Placement-targeted**—This is a popular one and can result in your getting an ad location all to yourself.

   Placement-targeted ads can appear only on pages in the Display Network. You choose a specific audience and site, or portion of a site, to target (these are called "managed placements"). If the ad group also has keywords, the keywords and placements will work together to determine where ads should appear. Keywords will continue to match your ads to placements through contextual targeting, and you can add your own placements to bid more when your ad appears on certain sites, or to limit your ad to appearing only on the placements you target.

The Top Five Things To Do If You Are Playing the Ad Game

1. **Capitalize the first letter of each word in your headline.** Google has tons of rules about caps, but so far you can still do this one, and it makes it appear more important. You can also add a ?, but Google doesn't like ! or $, so choose your symbols wisely or you will get

slapped (your ad gets pulled until you review it). Use your power words as you would for any advertising piece, and split-test various options. Million dollar tip: When adding your headline, don't forget to surround with {brackets} and mention a keyword for a jumpstart on that word. For example, {keyWord:Internet Marketing}.

2. **Track the results**. The two keys you will be looking for as your campaign rolls out are (1) cost per click (CPC)—the number of people who buy versus clicked through; (2) click-through rate (CTR)—the number of people who see it versus click through. Do it daily, and use this information for split-testing and tweaking, remembering to change only one thing at a time and test it.

3. **Go for the best position**. The ideal position is number four, which is the second down from the side bar. The position sequence goes top bar, top bar, side bar #3, and side bar #4. The side bar has a good chance of getting noticed, and by not being in the first position there is less chance of an accidental click through or compare click that costs you. By then they have also read a few and are getting ready to commit to going somewhere.

4. **Count your pennies**. To get the optimum position in the searches you have to bid for it. You pay every time someone clicks on your ad the amount that you bid. The key is to bid in odd numbers. Everyone bids 10 cents; you do 11 or 13 cents. Go in small increments, in odd numbers. Keep doing this until your ad appears on the front page.

5. **Some words cost a fortune**. You can spend $27 on a keyword and for some people this could be a bargain

depending on what their conversion rate is and the cost of what they are selling. Until then, you will have to get resourceful with your choices. You will really have to niche it down.

For example, let's say that you are in the dog-training business. That may be expensive to have, so you need to get niche specific; that is, "border collie dog training" might be cheaper, and still get good hits. You can use freekeywords.wordtracker.com to help you become the king of a niche, and not appear on page 10 of the search engines for something too generic or expensive. Your choice of keywords is critical to the success of your campaign. Be the king of a small niche until you can afford bigger.

Ten Places to Find Additional Keyword Possibilities

1. Misspellings of words. You can't use this in your ad, but you can use a misspelling in your bidding; for example, entreprenure for entrepreneur.

2. Go to the websites of your competitors to check out any meta tags and title they have on their own websites by going to their page; do a right click, and select view source. You'll see the keywords your competitors are using right at the top of the page.

3. Dictionary. Look for antonyms or synonyms to your keywords.

4. Amazon. Search your topic and check out book titles.

5. When you do a search, look at what the ads say that are in front of you.

6. Set a daily cost limit to an amount you can live with. Starting off can be scary. Until you have mastered putting together an ad and setting a bid price, the process may cost you some money during the learning curve, but if you do it in a gradient way, you won't get bankrupted in the first week. I made this mistake, jumped right in without knowing what I was doing, and I paid hundreds of dollars that I never even expected because I wasn't paying attention or tracking anything. I figured sales would simply happen to offset the costs.

7. Take a bull's-eye approach. Years ago we were all instructed to get thousands of keywords, plunk them into our account as a keyword or phrase, and then wait and see. This also cost me thousands of dollars. The problem was it was too hard to detect what caused the "click through and leave without buying or opting in." It could have been the keyword, sales page, landing page, or that visitors were searching for something so specific that my site didn't really match.

   So when doing a campaign, especially as a new-comer to the game, pick one keyword phrase and test just that for every ad in a campaign. Later you can add more as your experience grows.

8. Be dedicated. The key to a good ad campaign is to be committed to it. You need to check your results every day. You need to test the words, split-test by varying only one element, and then tweak it every few days always watching the CPC and CTR. When one keyword or phrase is doing poorly, you modify that, and compare it to the better-ranked one. This will get you

ultimately to the most effective ad. Once you have done this, you can add another campaign for the same product, changing the tone of it completely and see how this does. Then repeat the comparison to each ad and the other campaign until it gets better and better. Always track the ads by testing and tweaking.

9. Maintain a good attitude. You will more than likely spend some money and not make money as fast as you expected, or find yourself learning by trial and error. This is not a method for overnight success, but more of a finely tuned skill that when you master the method you will be able to dominate any market you choose with less and less cost.

10. Just do it. Despite all of the drawbacks in up-front learning and possible cost, just keep doing it, in smaller pieces if you have to. You need to appear on page one of Google in your niche, even if it is a small portion of your niche so that you can rule a market, and know that you are in the game. The only way you will really learn is by doing it.

Once you have mastered that universe, you can roll the same thing into other search engines, your e-mail, and offline promotion methods knowing you have a combination of keywords and a website that are working for you.

Overall, Google AdWords and Facebook ads are a powerful traffic magnet, and can definitely pay off as millions will attest. Get in the game, learn the rules, follow the rules, and master the art, and you will have conquered one of the big beasts that will result in success for your business for years to come.

The big difference in using a Facebook ad is you can get far more specific in your targeting. You can say you want males, age 45, who live in Colorado, and ski (that sounds almost like someone looking for a date). The targeting is incredible and powerful. To get started with Facebook ads, go to www.facebook.com/business/connect.

When considering the PPC field, make sure you also include Yahoo! (http://advertising.yahoo.com/), MSN Bing (http://advertising.microsoft.com/microsoft-adcenter), and Kanoodle (www.kanoodle.com).

Solo E-Mail and Ads

There are many newsletters out there with specific targeted audiences, and you can buy an ad or a solo e-mail that gets sent to their subscribers. Some things you want to check is: > target audience match > cost per person to send (it is a flat rate they will quote for a certain number of subscribers. If you divide it you'll be able to compare the cost per when evaluating the competition) > any testimonials or feedback posted regarding accuracy, rate of return > do one service at a time and see if it produced any results. If yes, repeat. If no, select another. > Choose ones where you don't have to sign up or you'll be flooded with offers. You can search on Google for ezine solo ads and look at some of these:

www.ezinead.net/index.php?pid=4

http://netgrannies.com/

www.adsmarket.biz/best-solo-ads.html

http://webstars2k.com/ezine7

DAY 24—PROVEN JOINT VENTURE BASICS

A joint venture (JV) is when two or more people or companies get together to undertake an economic activity. The sharing distribution is determined by both entities and the ultimate outcome is a win-win for everyone. Joint ventures are the fastest way to grow your list for little or no money, not to mention to make money. Generally it starts off that someone has a product, and someone else may have a list of possible purchasers. Together they can share the profit. If you have a product that is ready or a list just waiting, joint ventures are an economical way to accelerate sales. They give you instant access to a network of resources that could take you decades to reproduce, to a list that is usually hypersensitive to recommendations. Joint ventures create a scenario where you can earn more by doing less. They divide the work and get the word out faster. The best thing about JV relationships is that once you have partnered with someone, if that venture were successful, that person will be open to doing it again. You have a partnership for life in which you can both mutually grow. There are two sections we focus on: the steps to a successful joint venture and how to find joint venture partners. (For an expanded version of joint venture basics, visit www.JVCoachingClub.com for a free ebook.)

Five Easy Steps to a Successful Joint Venture

1. Start with one JV, and keep on looking. Don't put all your eggs into one basket. Continue to seek out new ways to create income.

2. If you are the one with the product, make sure it is high quality or you will be wasting people's time. You get one chance to make a first impression, and they may not

look at you again when you have gotten it together. Every shot needs to be your best.

3. Be forthright with your request but let the product, the sales letter, and the conversion rate talk for you. You should have already tested the market with your long copy sales letter site for your product and you should have seen a decent conversion on your sales! This is something you can use when pitching to the possible JV partners. Plus, they won't expose their database to anything that doesn't work so you will want to prove to them that it does.

4. Treat your JV partners like the gold that they are. Together you will be building a financial windfall, and you will want to continuously express your appreciation for their efforts even if it is just a matter that they push a key to their database that sends an e-mail you have created. The list is the key and if they have it, they are the gatekeeper.

5. Think long term. Have the next idea in mind or offer them an immediate benefit of sending to your database once it is built on their behalf. Even though you are giving them a hefty commission for their finger push, without them, there is no one to target. They take you from zero to 1,000 in four seconds flat.

Once you have ascertained that you are ready for a JV relationship, here is how you get them.

Five Steps to Getting Joint Venture Partners

1. **Market research**. Go to Google, Alexa, or Yahoo! and do a little market research. You want to search out your niche market and find people who have similar complementary

products to yours. You also want to see what kind of page rank they have on Alexa. Check traffic reports and manage the information into small workable quantities so that you can review it later. Check if they have an ezine or opt-in, take a look at their sales style, sales letter sites, opt-in methods, and overall approach to the marketplace. Make sure their philosophy matches yours.

2. **Review the data you have collected**. Decide who you would be interested in getting into a joint venture with. You may select more than one person to work with. Contact the person with a personalized e-mail that tells him or her about you and asks if there is anything you can do for them. Reciprocity is the most effective way to get joint venture partners. Personalize every e-mail, and offer them something first, because chances are they have hundreds of offers just like yours, and most won't listen if not approached properly. If they feel this is a cut-and-paste job, they will discard your e-mail quickly. The successful businesspeople you contact will not have time for "junk" e-mail. Offer to send them a free copy of the product that you want to promote through them. Show them the sales copy and the conversion numbers. (If you don't have the conversion numbers you may be able to convince them with just the copy of the product and sales copy.)

3. **Consider the commissions**. You need to offer your contacts a healthy profit on your product. The price will determine the margin in most cases. If you have a higher priced item you will want to consider going for around a 40 percent commission. If your product is a lower priced or regular ticket item ($197), you may consider going for the 50 to 70 percent margin, depending on the

purpose of the joint venture—is it money or list building. In the beginning, it may have to be list building.
Also work out the method of payment, for example,
PayPal, direct deposit. If you can control this aspect, all
the better. But many JV partners will do this and pay
you versus the other way around.

4. **Keep the communication open**. Develop the business
   relationship fully. Realize that the people you are
   working with are busy and may not have time to contact
   you. If you maintain that relationship it will benefit you
   because you might be able to do something else with
   them in the future. If you can talk to them over the
   phone, do this as much as possible. It takes it from
   a casual business venture to something more long term.

   Give them your Skype or Messenger and contact
   information. Let them know how they can reach you
   anytime during the joint venture cycle. Keep in contact
   through all of the steps and processes until you reach
   the final goal.

5. **Upon completion, make the payment quickly**. Send
   a personalized thank you in the form of a handwritten
   card. Again, personalization is the key here. Call them
   directly and say thank you. Yes, twice is always better
   than once. Ask them if it is okay if you keep them as
   a contact and give them a call once in a while and open
   the invitation for them to call you or e-mail you.

The key to joint ventures is to start building up your list of
prospects. It's best to focus on a list exchange with people
of comparable size. If you do approach someone with a 50,000-
member list and ask for an ad exchange when you only have
500 people, you will need to be creative and offer them

something more in return. By following these steps, you will succeed in the wonderful and lucrative world that is the lifeblood of fast-yielding profits and lists—joint ventures.

DAY 25—TELESEMINAR TRADE SECRETS AND WEBINAR WINS

A teleseminar is simply making a presentation to a bunch of people over the phone. A webinar is making a presentation online over the Internet. It is like a seminar in that you are educating people on some certain topic, and possibly even selling something, but it is done inexpensively and the next best thing to a live seminar. This is a great way to create a relationship with your prospects, and a great way to create a product in less than one hour, or make five to six figures in 90 minutes—and is one of my favorite things to do. Here are 32 secrets to success:

1. Decide to do it. Pick a date and make the presentation happen.

2. Pick the topic you are going to talk about and/or the product you want to sell.

3. Put together an e-mail invitation and prepare to send it out.

4. Put together the landing page where the e-mail will direct people so they can register. If you use a product such as GotoWebinar or wealth-webinars.com, then there is a registration process built in, but it still doesn't automatically get the subscriber from that system into your autoresponder so you will have to either import, enter manually, or find a resource or tool that will integrate them.

5. Prepare the autoresponder that will also send people the date, time, and call details. Don't give this to them on the thank-you page only; you want them to have this on their PC in case they lose the scrap of paper they may have just written the information on. (If this is your first teleseminar and you don't have a landing page, simply have them reply to the e-mail and respond directly or you'll have no way of reminding them on the day.)

6. If you expect fewer than 100 to attend, go to www.freeconferencecalling.com and get a free account, and hold a teleseminar.

7. If you think more than 100 that will attend, use a paid service such as www.GotoWebinar.com or www.Wealth-Webinars.com.

   Both of those options will cost you on a monthly basis; you just need to make sure then you use it enough to get your money's worth.

8. Print out the instructions from the service you have chosen, and practice them so that you can smoothly operate the mute, unmute, turn chimes off, block new callers, check the number on the call, record, and play with all of the features.

9. If you are using the free service you may need to record the teleseminar yourself on your own computer. Practice doing this. I recommend that the computer that will record it be separate from the one you are on. Have another PC call in to the teleseminar, go in as a listener (not as a host like you are—it reduces feedback and echo), and start recording.

10. If you are using a paid service, just know how to use it.

11. Send out a voice reminder just before the teleseminar is about to start—for example, about 15 minutes—contact markettouchmedia.com or voiceshot.com to send out an automated phone reminder. You can also do the same thing with your autoresponders and send out a broadcast e-mail. Even if people haven't registered on your list, you can use this to remind them the presentation is coming up, and provide the log-in codes. The phone reminder is a paid service, but if you are doing a Joint Venture call where someone is coming on to sell, it could be worth it because the more people you have on the call, the more money you could generate.

12. Tuesday and Thursday are the best seminar days around 6 P.M. PST, 9 P.M. EST, but remember that you are also competing with the best for those slots. I do mine on Wednesday.

13. Don't wing it. Know your topic, know what you are going to say, have it scripted, rehearse it, and practice staying on track. If you were going on stage you wouldn't go unprepared and the same goes for your teleseminar or webinar. Just because people can't see you doesn't mean it's okay to just ruffle through your papers or log onto the Internet for guidance. Be ready to wow them, rehearse the closing, put together a spectacular deal they can't refuse, and you will have a success on your hands.

14. Be pleasant, smile (attendees can feel it), show you care, give them lots of fantastic free information, help

them, guide them, and then at the very end, for just a few minutes, wrap it up with your pitch. Be passionate, and make it not about you or your product, but how this will change their lives.

15. Remember that people will leave and hang up, not take you up on your offer, but that is okay because someone else will stay, and buy, and that is who you need to focus your attention on.

16. Practice makes perfect. Practice again, and again and again, until it is like talking to your family on the phone, only you're doing it with friends you can't hear.

17. Remember that you can't hear the attendees, because you want to put your system on mute or else you will get tons of feedback, but they can hear you. So get rid of background noise—the dog barking if you're at home, your kids. You need to do this from a place where there will be no interruptions, including your cell phone, so turn it off.

18. Once you have done one presentation, do them all of the time. This is where you get someone's attention while they listen to you, as you provide some information and sell them something, too. If you haven't sold anything that week, get a presentation going. Just because it is last minute, doesn't mean it won't work.

19. Promote products by highlighting the benefits attendees will walk away with—not the features of your product. Take on a "What's in it for me?" attitude from attendees' perspective, and start writing. This is the content that will be used in your invitation and on your landing page.

20. Don't wait until the very end to talk about what you are going to pitch. There is a sweet spot in the middle of the presentation at about minute 25, where many may have to leave—drop a hint at this point about what you are going to be offering, give a website or the product name. Integrate into the pitch by having a leading question or solution to a problem, and then say that you'll talk more about this at the end—it may be enough to keep those people on.

21. After the teleseminar or webinar, send another auto-responder thanking people for attending and sending them to a web page that contains your offer in a sales page web format. Send this to everyone who registered and even those that didn't with a preamble such as "For those of you who were on the call, and even those of you who couldn't make it, there is still time to take advantage of this exclusive subscriber offer."

22. If you are going to open this up for a question free-for-all at the end, don't use the unmute option because this will result in the feedback and noise again, but use the "hand raising" option, which will display the phone number, and you can unmute that one caller, and invite the person to speak based on the first three digits of the phone number.

23. Spend the first seven minutes of the call giving your background and history, because this is when the stragglers are still connecting, and you don't want them to miss the good stuff.

24. If you want to get fancy, send people a brief agenda or handout they can use during the event to fill in answers

or serve as a workbook during the event so they can get the maximum out of the presentation.

25. Don't be worried about the number of people who attend, especially if you are just starting out. The number could fool you, and if out of the 60 that pre-registered only four show up, then focus on those four and make it a nice intimate meeting. Even if there is just one person out there, talk as if there are a 100. Practice makes perfect, and use every opportunity to do just that.

26. The biggest failure you can have in a teleseminar or webinar is that you don't hold one. You'll miss out on a really great way to build a relationship with your prospects, and possibly sell them.

27. Have fun. This is you reaching out to people who need your product, and it's about your wanting to give information that will help them. This is a good thing, and should not make you feel nervous or worried. Enjoy the journey with your new friends, and they will enjoy sharing it with you.

28. If you close a sale on your first event, then celebrate. This is a fantastic testimony to your product, to you, and to the great job you just did. Whether it is a $17 ebook, or a $1,700 training package, it is just the start, and you have now done something that others haven't.

29. Check in to the seminar 15 minutes before it is meant to start. You want to be the first one there. Then wait and listen. The chimes will ring when others are coming in. In the beginning this is fun to listen to because the chimes mean that your invitation worked

and people are coming. Then as they log in, say hi, welcome them, tell them you're going to get started in just a few minutes, and that you'll turn off the chimes shortly and that the chimes are other people coming on (and let them hear that they aren't the only ones there). Then tell them that you will be muting the call soon and that you will no longer be able to hear the chimes. Then do it, tell them that you've done it, and start into the introduction at the start time of the event. Don't sit and wait around for slackers; reward those who logged in on time.

30. If you don't think you can talk into a telephone and have nobody talk back, then enlist a friend to do it with you. It is so easy. Have them ask you the questions, you answer them, they react, and so on. It is easy, and fun.

31. Be natural. Even though you are working from a script, don't make it sound that way. Follow the points as a reminder and then say it like you would in a normal conversation. Glance to make sure that all of the issues have been covered, and then move to the next one.

32. Be organized. Have all of the information in front of you, how to manage the call, your script/notes, start to record the call before it starts, and then give the attendees what you would want to receive if you were on the other end.

A teleseminar or webinar is a great and valuable tool to keep in touch with your prospects and even better, your clients. So do these presentations, do them often, and have fun while you are doing it. It will become as natural as talking to a friend with the rewards of a sale or future sale from the relationships you are building.

Then, turn the presentation into a product for sale, cut out chunks of audio for podcasting, and you've created a great way to also do something once, and make money at it.

Day 26—YouTube and Video Sites

Google knows a good thing when it sees it or else why would it pay $1.65 billion for YouTube, which is a video-sharing project that has turned into the number two search engine in the world. Did you ever wonder how you can ride the wave of success at YouTube? The best ratings and editors' picks are going to people from all walks of life. Everything from "Psy and Gangnam Style," "Charlie Bit My Finger," and "Tootin' Bathtub Baby Cousins" have a huge following and are among the most viewed videos on YouTube to date.

What makes these videos successful? Fun, fresh, unusual, weird, there is no end to what people want to watch. Many people are just being themselves. People create their own personal type of production that is based on their personality. Each clip is typically three to five minutes in length depending on the material. Make sure that you are creating quality material and posting about two times a week. Your clips should be approximately one- to three-minutes long. If you are going to do an upcoming project, take about two minutes to describe it as a teaser and send people to your landing page, post it, and go! If you are planning on going into depth about something, I have noticed that the average length does not exceed 10 minutes, so think infomercial with less hype and more heart.

Word-of-mouth advertising is the best way to get people to come to your video blog. Most people who do well said that they didn't do anything to actively market. They just wrote down ideas, filmed them, and posted them to the site. Then, they told their friends who told others, which created hype. Justin Bieber, Grayson Chance, and smosh were nobodies before YouTube. Now Justin is a household name, Grayson was signed by Ellen, and smosh has offers including MTV—old-fashioned viral marketing at its finest.

You can also embed the video code and stick it on your own website and blog. If you do this you will get noticed by the visitors of your own site, and other sites, too. Grant others free access to copy and distribute and post, and you will get results similar to the article marketing concept.

A *share button* is also another viral feature that keeps the message going. It is great for getting extra free exposure and people can e-mail the link of the clip to their friends, who can do the same to other friends. If you make sure your message is strong or unique enough that people will use it to teach others, and have your website address somewhere on it, it is a surefire way to encourage a viral effect.

Focus on your unique selling proposition (USP). People who have been marketing their business know the USP will help them stand out. The common thread that the popular channels have is that each is unique in its presentation. This goes back to being yourself, with a twist. Make sure you keep in mind your "brand identity" so that when people see you they don't even have to look at the name. Take a look at what is on Spotlight, Trending, and Featured, and figure if there is a way you can do something similar, yet unique.

Videos give you a chance to build a rapport with your audience. People will appreciate the opportunity to hear you "live" whenever they want. You will be able to get your products out to them more quickly by providing demonstrations of how to apply the product to their lives.

Are you ready to take on YouTube? Then upload your video and copy the code and add it to every other applicable site you own.

Want to be able to send video e-mails?

Create your video, upload it to YouTube, and send the link or embed it in the e-mail to your subscribers. Then you have created a free instant video e-mail. Even better is to create your own community by asking your subscribers to join YouTube directly to your community. Once they have done that they will not only have a direct link to you, but they will also be able to join forces with you to create a more expansive market base.

If someone looks at your profile and sees your videos, you may have just made another customer. And what did you do? You sent an e-mail asking your subscribers to become part of YouTube. This is viral marketing at its easiest. There are so many ways that you can use YouTube in your marketing. You need a hint of creativity, some ingenuity, and a little time. With a camera and the right software you will be well on your way to creating one of the easiest marketing strategies people have seen. The biggest tip here is to take the marketing you know, look at all the old marketing tips, tricks, and techniques and apply them.

Think how you can use YouTube. Then make it happen. Then make sure you sign up for DailyMotion.com and Vimoe .com and upload everything you do here, too.

You don't need to get fancy—if you have a webcam on your PC, you're ready. For recommended video software see that section in Chapter 4.

eBay and Auctions

eBay is the world's largest and most trusted auction house with sellers offering page ranks for sale.

I do not talk about eBay from a true sell-your-product perspective or how to build an eBay business. The angle I come from is how to use eBay as a traffic-generation tool. One of the latest trends is to capture the traffic from well-established ranking sites such as Google Page Rank 7, PR 6, PR 5, and PR 4, and promote your site, sell your products, and leverage the link. Combine this with back link and page-rank opportunities, and you have yourself a potential goldmine. You can expose your products to a completely different audience, and bypass the hard work and simply buy your way into a good page rank.

Page Ranks

Most people know that it is not easy to obtain and maintain a solid page rank without having to work hard at it. If you are bidding and purchasing on a ranked site you will definitely want to make sure to check the rank with other tools to ensure that you are getting a real value for your money. To check a page rank go to www.alexa.com.

What does it take to get a decent ranking on a website? It takes a lot of work, such as links and content. Links mean not only the quality of links you have on your site, but also the quantity. Your links not only have to come from other high-ranking sites, but the sites must also be relevant and relate to your specific niche. This could mean a lot of work for any webmaster. You would have to find the relevant websites, check their ranking and contact them, and hope they will link to you.

Someone Else Does the Work for You   Not everyone has the time or even ability to focus on increasing or establishing his or her page ranks. This is why eBay page-ranking auctions have become a viable option. The work is already done for you, the links have been established, the ranks are established, and they will require little to no additional effort on your part. The only real exception of effort is to design your website and get it up and running if that hasn't already been done.

How Does It Work?   Getting started is simple. All you need is an eBay account and you are ready to go. Getting an eBay account is free, and you can use it for bidding on page rank buys, and for selling all of that stuff from your attic or garage if you choose to do so in the future. Type in page rank in the search function and take a look at the different auctions available. You can find a variety of ranked pages available; pages ranked 5 or 6 seem to be the most popular. The next thing you want to do is check for site relevancy to your own.

Once you spot one you want, you can bid or if they have the "Buy Now" button, simply go for it ($9.99 is a good deal). Right now, people are purchasing these ranked pages and placing an inexpensive item for sale on them. Then they are driving this traffic to their real site, in which they offer their real products and services by listing all of the contact and promotion information in the "About Me" section. Once you get people to buy it is easy to invite them into your autoresponder system, where you can continue the relationship as well.

You can also use this new page rank for generating an opt-in list. You can prompt people to sign up to receive your newsletter or to offer more information on what you have.

You can get started with free accounts from www.eBay.com or www.ebid.net.

Mobile Marketing—Now or Later?

With 5.1 billion mobile phone users, mobile-ready websites have become a requirement by Google in satisfying the latest search engine protocols, especially for searches from a mobile phone. But many people confuse being mobile ready with mobile marketing, so this chapter explains the difference and gets you prepared for both.

What Is Mobile Marketing? Mobile marketing involves communicating with the consumer via mobile device (i.e., smart phone) to make searching easier, buying faster, and introducing people to a new relationship-building model. It additionally includes reaching this audience with a mobile-ready website, and simplifying the search with QR codes.

A QR code stands for *quick response* and it allows users to scan the code and be taken to a website location that can serve unlimited marketing messages.

You use an app on your mobile phone to scan the QR code. If you want to create one easily for your landing page or master site go to www.GetAFreeQRCode.com.

There are many apps to read a QR code. *Scan* is free and the one I use is for the iPhone. From a marketing standpoint there are nine major types of mobile marketing, such as SMS (short message service) and mobile advertising, but the key for business owners is to start by getting your current website *mobile ready*.

Mobile Marketing Is **Not** *a Trend*   Mobile marketing is *not* a trend, it is a stable method of reaching your audience, but more importantly, it is a mandatory medium that must be addressed. Ignoring this topic is like ignoring the Internet years ago.

Mobile marketing is where Google, social media, Amazon, eBay, and *all* the major sites are putting their focus—so if you want to stay or even get ahead of the curve right now, you need to know this more than any other topic out there.

- Mobile searchers are *hot* buyers—81 percent are looking to buy something *now* and 50 percent buy on the spot.

- Ninety-five percent of mobile owners use it to search locally.

- There are 6.9 billion people in the world and 5 billion have a mobile phone. This shatters the 2.1 billion users who search via the Internet.

- You can choose to do it—and *make money*—or ignore it and *lose* money and *customers*.

Testing Mobile Readiness

Your website is *not* automatically mobile ready.

Figure 6.1 shows what a typical site will look like when you test it—a mini-squashed version of your site, and you figure you are good to go because it displayed.

However, as far as Google is concerned, you don't exist.

To Be Mobile Ready, Your Site Has To Satisfy Four Criteria

1. **Speed**—It must load fast.

2. **Size**—Fonts and text must be geared toward fat fingers.

Figure 6.1 Testing for Mobile Readiness

3. **Ease of navigation**—Simple and easy to get the information people want.

4. **Touch integration**—To e-mail, phone, location, and direction.

Go to www.tracyrepchuk.com/mobiletest and type in your website name.

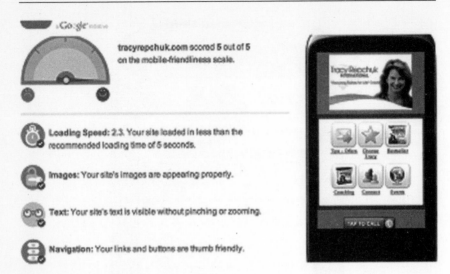

Figure 6.2   Mobile Readiness Revealed

You will see what it looks like and that it is probably not mobile ready. Then I want you to type in my domain at that site: www.TracyRepchuk.com.

If you type my domain from your mobile phone and your computer, you will see two different sites displayed.

Then I want you to type in my domain at that site: www .TracyRepchuk.com. You will see that my site satisfies all the criteria, and what it should look like (see Figure 6.2).

So how can you make your site mobile ready? The key elements of your site need to be identified.

You can see from my site, which has many options, that I chose:

- Opt-in: Get the visitor's name and e-mail address.
- Briefly about me: > Link to Amazon to buy my book > Brief description of top coaching programs.

- Connect: These are my social media links.

- Events: This talks about where I am appearing next.

Tap to Call: Dials Your Office Directly

The key is to focus on the fastest ways to get in touch with you, find you, locate you on a map if you have a physical location, and buy from you. If people can find you, they'll either show up or call.

But a bad mobile experience will cost you customers forever. It is now becoming a make or break moment for your business.

How to Leverage Mobile Technology

You need to optimize the Google SEO regulations that have been put in place, and ensure your place at the top of the search engine rankings. Without a mobile site, Google will start to penalize you.

Google SEO = customers, which in turn = money and sales. It's a marketing medium that can't be ignored, and if you want to skyrocket past your competition, get in now, get established, and dominate your market.

- Dominate the search engines.

- Connect with customers instantly via phone, text, or e-mail.

- Integrated built-in payment system.

- Automatically build a list of hungry buyers.

- Mobile phones are always carried, they are personal and always on.

- SMS advertising is the fastest, most convenient way to directly hit your target customers.

- There are different stages of development.

- Get your current site mobile ready—this isn't an option: > create a communication method using SMS technology to push messages to prospects and clients.

- Focus on methods to dominate your keywords with Google to optimize searches.

- Get an app for clients and prospects to engage them.

The quick answer: Mobile-ready websites—*now*. Mobile marketing—*later*. Get your product funnel in place first.

If you need help check out www.MobileSolutionsForBiz.com.

Getting It Done for You

So we have progressed through many steps, what you need to do, in what order, and that is one of the major issues newcomers to Internet marketing face—what to do when. You might be thinking, this is all very technical—I can't do that. Well, that's okay. If you know what needs to be done, you can pay someone else to do it. And before you say "I can't afford to pay anyone, I'm not making any money yet," think again. You can get people for $3 or $7 per hour. They will make your videos for $12. You can get a landing page for $27. The pages or videos may not be perfect, but you don't have to get it right, you just have to get it going. You can improve, test, tweak, and constantly adjust as your skills grow, but the faster you get something up there, the faster money can come in the door. Here are the locations I use for outsourcing:

www.Fiverr.com—Good for small quick tasks

www.Elance.com—Best prices

www.GetaFreeLancer.com—Best delivery

www.EasyOutsourcingNow.com—Personal team

CHAPTER 6 ACTION PLAN

- Set up a Google AdWord campaign with a unique keyword niche, and continue to get familiar with test and tweak, and how it works.
- Find JV partners.
- Book a date and do a teleseminar or webinar.

CHAPTER 7

Maximizing Your Marketing Funnel

Day 27—Know Your Statistics

There are tons of statistics you can track as you grow, but when you are just starting out there are only three you need to be watching.

1. **Money in**. This might sound simple—all of the website and ad tracking is wonderful, but if you don't have a weekly income coming in the door, you need to address this fast. You need to focus on a sales campaign every week. If that's not bringing money in, the more outflow you have, whether e-mail or ads, the more inflow you will get. It is simple math. So no matter what you track in your business, the cash balance comes first.

2. **Google AdWords**. If you have this, make sure you have used the insert tags throughout your web pages so that you can track the conversion rates. Follow these to improve by testing and tweaking. If you don't have AdWords activated, track the website conversion of visitors to opt-ins from web stats.

3. **Page hit stats and bounce rates**. You can activate Google Analytics within your Google account, add the code to your web page, and then in one location within Google you can track critical pages of your different domains or campaigns, and you will get a report.

There are a few methods to monitor web and e-mail activity. They all serve a different purpose, and some provide overview while others give you the detail you may need. Take a look below at some of your options, and decide what is best for your promotion and business plan.

Website Statistics

Most ISPs have detailed logs of your web activity, everything from monthly statistics, daily statistics, day of week statistics, hourly statistics, most page views, and most visits. Then they can provide general statistics such as: top 10 files by number of hits, top 10 files by volume, complete file statistics, top 10 most frequently requested 404 files (errors), complete 404 file not found statistics, and a breakdown of domain origins by country. Then you get page-by-page statistics, hits, keywords, and more.

This is sometimes in a raw format, but if you have done an e-mail blast or just put up a new banner someplace, this is a great place to come and see if the web hits have increased.

For general statistics you can look at the referrer's report, which details how people are finding your site—links from other websites (possibly an advertising campaign), various e-mail or newsletter sponsorships or articles, search engines, and more. It even provides you with the URL of the referring site so you can see exactly where your hits are coming from. By paying close attention to this report, you can determine if the ad campaign has been successful (compare the percentage of hits coming from other websites and follow the referring links to see precisely who is sending you hits) or whether you need to boost your marketing efforts.

It also allows you to monitor the success of on-site promotions.

Try setting up another page within your site that details a monthly promotion. Make your visitors aware of the promotion by advertising it on your homepage or sending an e-mail. Then watch your referrer's report to see how well the promotion does. The report will detail which link (e-mail, homepage, etc.) is sending the most hits to your special promotion page so you can determine which format is most preferred by your audience and most effective for your site.

You usually have to display a banner with these services.

Set Up Separate Websites for Ads and E-Mail Promotions

If the campaign is large, you may even want to set up an entirely new website to monitor the progress and flow through of the ad and each page. Most ISPs allow you to set up "subdomains." These are domain names that go to your original account (for example, www.innersurf.com), but when the user invokes the subdomain name (for example, www.remotedesk.net) it is rerouted to a subdirectory on your site (that you must set up), and it looks like a completely new site, with new statistics for specialized monitoring. Sometimes these subdomains can cost a few dollars a month, but they are a great way to know exactly the results of an ad campaign, and are nowhere near the expense of setting up an actual new original domain name site with a new ISP.

Use HTML Forms and Separate E-Mail Addresses

When you create a banner ad or send an e-mail blast, you need to monitor the progress, so set up either a completely new page that receives the click-throughs from that ad, or an HTML form where they can make some sort of request that is also unique to the campaign. This form is then sent to a specific e-mail address that once again is unique to the campaign. With our ISP, we can have unlimited e-mail addresses so that we control the setup ourselves, and this is really convenient when it comes to seeing the actual results of a marketing campaign.

Tracking Tags

Tracking tags help you track the source of opt-ins from the landing or website page through the autoresponder system. Make sure you activate this in every campaign within your autoresponder system. These are just some basic statistics for you to start off with.

Day 28—The Marketing Funnel Product Model

The marketing funnel is progressive steps to getting people to spend ever-increasing amounts of money on autopilot, over and over and over again. It is the big picture marketing technique that keeps you focused, and I refer to it as the Millionaire by Design chart from Chapter 4. The principles apply to any product, but when you can create something, set up an automated sales cycle, and walk away while cash fills your bank account; this gives you the freedom to do whatever you want with your time. It gives you freedom of choice. You do it once, and repeat it for every idea you have.

Keep in mind that although it is often shaped like a funnel, that doesn't that mean someone can't cut in at a higher-priced item. It just means the majority of your flow will occur this way. I recommend that you introduce visitors early to a higher-priced program (i.e., I go from my $24.95 book to coaching program— "Acquire to Leverage Levels"). It's a big jump, but you get the people who are ready right away, and the others will work up to it.

The market funnel has various stages generically called the *front end*, *upsell*, and *back end*, but throughout the progressions there can be a few gradient steps:

- **Acquire**. This is the place where the visitors come across your site and are curious enough about what you have. They see you have packed so much value and delivery in abundance that they're "willing to lose" that amount of money to see if your delivery matches your promise. This is in the free-to-$47 range.

- **Nurture stage**. If your last stage delivered in abundance, this is where buyers expect to receive another product similar to that and they expect at least one element that if implemented would prove to be true and work. The $97 area is where you can introduce affiliates and invite joint venture opportunities to your model.

- **Comfort stage**. Clients have gotten a few things from you that have proven to be reliable and work. They haven't invested too much yet, but they can see you deliver what you say and are starting to get comfortable with you in the $197 to $497 range.

- **Trust stage**. Clients trust you and are expecting to recoup what they pay by applying the principles you teach or knowledge you share in the $497 to $1,497 range.

- **Reward stage**. This is a stage where buyers expect to make a certain amount beyond what they have spent, such as in the $1,997 to $2,997 range. The mentor stage can start here.

- **Leverage stage**. This is where the buyer has become hypersensitive to what you say and offer, they buy it, they are dedicated to you, and are at the higher end of your funnel. They are hoping that you are part of their leverage strategy. The range is $3,497, $5,497, $9,997, $14,497, $19,997, and up.

- **Peer stage**. This is the stage where your clients have evolved to a successful level in their own right. They are learning at a rate where they can teach you things as well. This level consists of more intimate coaching, training, mentoring, and business-growth strategies; you take their phone call anytime, you are a reliable confidant to guide and keep them on track. This is also the stage where you are earning consistent cash, and are becoming a viable joint venture at a partner level.

- **Inner circle stage**. This is where you, your client, upper level joint venture partners are no longer paying each other for strategies, you simply work mutually exclusive, yet together, sharing ideas and concepts, accelerating each other's gains.

WARNING

If at any point you lose faith in your ability to achieve and attract what you want, simply go back to Chapter 1, review your goals, and get your mind-set back intact, and then finish what you started.

The funnel will vary price-wise and level-wise depending on where your status is in the industry. When you're at the top like Dan Kennedy, Jay Abraham, and others, the entry level could be far greater, but you can see how the progression goes.

You move a prospect through the levels to the ultimate location where you are, and together you both continue rising to higher levels of wealth and enrichment.

The really neat thing is that even though the number of people seems to be reducing as it goes through the funnel, your profits increase and the amount of work required decreases. It is an inversion process, especially because at the very top levels it usually doesn't involve any JV or affiliate referrals, and all the profits are yours.

It is a fun game, regardless of where you are, whether a mentee, mentor, or just starting out. When you understand how it is played, you get a very good certainty on where you are, what you need to do in order to progress, where you are aiming, and the people you need in order to get there.

REMINDER

You don't want to limit the funnel to just one type of product. You want to eventually have *most* of them. The key is to have one, deliver it, and then move on and repeat the same type of product, or add another and go deeper down the funnel.

DAY 29—THE FRONT END

The front end of the marketing chain is like a wide-mouthed funnel where hundreds and thousands of people pour in to check out your offerings. Now the subscriber can enter at any level, but in general the subscriber/visitor goes through a general progression. Visitors could have come from anywhere in the traffic cycle, but they usually land at the front door and start looking at what you do.

This is the *Acquire Stage*.

Because visitors don't know you, you need to build a relationship with them and offer them something to prove that you have good information that they can use. There are two ways to start them off at this stage, and that is by offering something for free such as: a report, ebook, or subscription to an ezine where they will continue to get great information over time. Either way, whatever they have done by this point has usually cost nothing or very little.

Once visitors have entered into the world of what you do and have, you will start to build the relationship through autoresponders, teleseminars, or seminars. Then, they will probably buy their first front-end product. The price of the front end varies depending on where they found you. If it was a normal autoresponder cycle, it could vary from $17 to $97. If they attended a teleseminar, the same price range may apply, with perhaps an upper range up to $497. If their first point of contact was a seminar, this can range from about $97 to $1,997. Wherever the front end is for you, your job now is to make sure they are satisfied (using surveys), and that you keep in touch, constantly moving people toward the next level of the funnel.

For each price point of the front end you will also need to consider the bonus bundle that goes with it. The average bonus bundle is four times the price of the product, at a minimum usually of $150 in freebies. If people bought in at $17, the bonus bundle needs to be about a value of $150. If they came in at $497, you're looking at $1,700, and at $1,997, you need to add some huge bonus value that will usually entail a half-hour private phone session or some other exclusive feature.

The Comfort Level

This is the next flow through the funnel. Depending on where visitors landed in your autoresponder system (because the starting price point of each entry level varies), they will now be presented with that next step.

By this point, people may have already bought a few things from you that have proven to be reliable and work, or they know you by reputation. They haven't invested too much yet, but they can see you deliver what you say, and are starting to get comfortable with you in the $197 to $497 range.

Each step has to constantly keep in mind the rising crescendo of information and value, and what people are looking for now is definite results.

The Trust Factor

Once the trust factor has been established, a stage of hypersensitive reactivity to what you have to say and offer occurs. This means that you are now at a level where purchasers are expecting that what they buy, they will recoup by applying the principles you teach or the knowledge you share.

This stage opens the door easily to the reward, leverage, and beyond levels, where people will start to become a partner and prospect for life, providing you continue to deliver at a high standard of quality and recoverability.

DAY 30—THE BACK END

The back end is the reason that most marketers do what they do, and design the structure the way they do. It is the funnel at its finest. This is the holy grail of all sales, and sits there waiting for the relationship to build to a point where it culminates toward the top-of-the-mountain purchase. The cost of this varies, and can range from $2,497 to $24,977, depending on what you offer. Most marketers take the steps and prices you have just reviewed and start at the back end when designing. Decide what is going to be at the back end, and then build toward the front to step and ease a purchaser toward it. Think of what you would want to see, and what purchasing gradients you would expect if it were you. The trip to the back end has quite likely been a trip of multiple product purchases, and a teleseminar or seminar face-to-face meet, or it was from word of mouth and a reputation that simply demands what you have for a specific audience. However people got here, you need to put your effort into what this is, design this in full benefit-spilling details, and take a look again now at what you decided was your front end, and each step in between to make sure the stages feed each other and align with a purpose or evolution toward a higher goal fulfilled.

Then pile on the bonuses and member-only features.

Examples of back ends include training, mentoring, coaching, and consulting. These are the most common. If there is one thing I have noticed about the Internet marketing gurus and their back ends is that regardless of the price, they still over-deliver and if you do whatever is demanded of the program, the mentor will want you to be satisfied, and will do what needs to be done to guarantee it. The Internet is a small market, and an unhappy customer can go a long way to destroy years of nurturing.

Then give the biggest guarantee you can, and don't leave your purchasers stranded. Be confident of your power and abilities to help someone and claim your dreams.

So regardless of where you are in your funnel, if you have sold multiple copies of your back end, make sure you make a new back end, and keep going up that ladder until you can't go any higher. For the back end there needs to be no end in sight. Once you have closed one person, be ready with the next level.

Three Successful Actions to Moving People to the Back End

1. Build trust. Every product that led them to the back end needs to have been delivered in such abundance that they know that whatever they spend will be recouped.

2. Your entry-level products need to be inexpensive and treated as part of the sales and lead generation cycle, and don't contain sales pitches for your next level, but deliver whatever you said it was going to.

3. Work the marketing funnel, always adding more in the front from free, to free, to free, to entry, to comfort, to trust, to premium, and premium plus, and platinum, and remember that your funnel doesn't stop at your initial design—that was merely a template to grow from.

Simple Surveys

Surveys are an integral part of the success of any business. They are a way of asking potential clients or current customers how they feel about something. It takes the guesswork out of a situation, and lets you add certainty to future plans, changes, additions, or decisions.

You can use surveys for things such as finding out if a product is needed and wanted or for checking out how someone found your site. An exit survey can find out why the person is leaving without opting-in or buying. You can do satisfaction rating surveys, and ask about any aspect of your business cycle.

A survey is a great way to communicate and to get feedback from your visitors and clients. It is also another way to keep in touch. Doing a survey is easier than ever before. With free services such as www.surveymonkey.com it is easy to get results and improve your company and products.

When you get your feedback from a survey, you can integrate any considerations, barriers, or issues encountered and reported, and address them head on. Teach visitors how to overcome them with your autoresponders, or what can be done to avoid them. Feedback puts you at cause, and allows you to be proactive in your effort to grow and improve.

Make sure surveys are a part of your business and communication cycle, and simply put them automatically anywhere you can.

Day 31—Your Corporate Future

Hopefully, you have read the entire book. I don't expect you to have finished every single item in 31 days, but you should have familiarized yourself with each concept and understand how it works within your strategy and niche, and how and when you need to implement it.

The key to your successful corporate and Internet marketing future lies with you. You control you. You make the decisions. You take action or not. You listen to friends or not. You work harder to get it going, or not. You can't blame anyone, because that puts you at effect. You can't succeed if you are at effect. You can succeed if you are being cause. Mistakes may happen. You hope they don't, but when they do, keep going forward, and take the lesson that will prevent it from happening again. Don't ever label anything as a failure; it is simply something you tried that didn't work. The failure is *not* trying.

What you are starting sounds small, but in essence, it is a business. It may just be a product, or service, but when you apply all of the concepts, especially the multiple streams of income, you need to get serious about setting it up properly.

Once you start to make more than $20,000 on the Internet, you should incorporate and get in touch with an accountant. There are great places to incorporate for a low price at www.amerilawyer.com or www.LegalZoom.com.

If you're not from the United States, look into Delaware or Nevada corporations to see if you can take advantage of those offerings, or simply incorporate where you are. Talk to someone on the phone versus just ordering, though, because there are a few things you need to know that can save you tons of money such as Sub-Chapter S, which is a great tax savings strategy. In addition, you can connect with companies such as prepaid legal and get some terrific advice and legal/business help when you need it for a low cost

You need to think like a business, which means that each week you have to sit down on Monday and say, "What am I going to sell this week?" Whether you come up with a special offer on your own stuff or sell an affiliate product, you have to try to sell something to your subscribers every week. If blast e-mails aren't working, remember to do a teleseminar and really let subscribers know what they need, and why.

Lastly, when the business starts to grow, two things will happen. If you work for someone else (aka a job) the time will come to leave and assume your role in your business full time. It may come by your choice or your employer's if you take too long to make up your mind, but either way make a decision that you are going to make this work, and do whatever it takes to create the life you always dreamed of.

> **TIP**
>
> Automate, outsource, and work your vision.

Trends and Trappings

Internet marketing never sleeps and is constantly evolving. That means keeping up with what's hot and what interesting trends and topics seem to be emerging:

Pinterest and Instagram: Just like Google+ and Twitter of years ago, these are the new up and comers. Secure your account until they fit into your marketing plan.

SMS (short message service) is text messages sent to a cell phone. Because of the reduction in e-mail opening and efficiency, the next method being explored is having people opt-in to a landing page that sends messages to people's cell phones. Tests show a great open rate right now, but it is also currently expensive. So get your foundation in first, then do this if you are a speaker or attend live events frequently.

The cloud: Cloud computing as means of increasing capacity without investing in new infrastructure has become the holy grail of modern enterprises. In small business situations it can be great for backup, but unlike tools like dropbox.com, it doesn't reduce the speed of your computer. Still having some growing pains with security, the cloud is something to keep your eye on, considering that in most cases if your data are gone, so is your business. Examples are Google Drive.

Creating an ATM Cash Machine

Once you have gotten your foundation in place, established yourself in the market place, automated your communication, and are earning money consistently, it's time to take your core knowledge and leverage it wherever possible.

Multiple Streams of Income   There are two methods you can use to get more money in without more of your time, and that is setting up an affiliate program and/or hiring salespeople. Then adding more products from your existing line that are compatible to your core offerings, with upsells (i.e., people buy one thing, but if they want these extra things, add this for more money) and downsells (a lesser offer).

In general, though, creating multiple streams of income involves rinse, repeat, and spread across another product. You simply need to duplicate landing page, sales page, and the power of blogs across your next idea. To turn your product and soon company into an ATM machine, you need to do 10 things:

1. Select a market you can make money at: niche research.

2. Ensure that systems can be created to automate it. For Internet marketing that power comes from autoresponders.

3. Create the product the market wants.

4. Plan your marketing funnel from the back end first.

5. Plan the stages through the funnel, and remember your bonuses.

6. Keep the traffic coming by applying all of the tools you can.

7. Set up an affiliate program and have a sales army sell for you.

8. Add multiple streams of income by recommending similar products.

9. Find joint venture opportunities.

10. Repeat, bring out a new product, add more products, and continue to automate as much as possible. Internet marketing is an amazing field once you have mastered it, and I am hoping you start to apply the "31 Days to Millionaire Marketing Miracles," and really start to create the wealth you have always dreamed of.

This is like a diet. Do a bit every day. Make it a new habit. Keep it up, add more on top of a working foundation—and celebrate your victories.

It's up to you now!

Being the Maker of Your Miracles

Well, it's 31 days later, and are the millions rolling in??

No, but believe it or not, it isn't the point—*yet*! This isn't about a million dollars in 31 days; it is about putting together the foundation to be able to achieve it. Remember, the gurus took years to earn their first million, but when they did, the rest came easy because they had the steps they needed in place to grow and repeat—which is what you should have, too. You have to work this plan over and over to tighten, tweak, and stabilize.

You posted your goals at the beginning of this journey, and if you followed each step, every day, you either educated yourself or familiarized yourself with a new concept, or if you were already familiar, implemented that concept to integrate your goals and Internet marketing strategy. Rome was not built in a day, and most Internet marketing empires aren't either.

It is a process where if you have the blueprint as I have just provided, and you keep putting those pieces in tighter, better, and working them until it is a finely tuned automobile, capable of running itself, then that is where the real payoff begins. That is where your computer turns into an ATM machine.

Once every step is done, and completed, and running on automatic—you can sit back and decide what part you want to continue to play in this specific project. You can still be the one-person band or a group if that is the case. You can continue to repeat these steps for different products or services through your marketing funnel, and/or you can start to hire a staff and turn it into a real business. You can get people responsible for the various aspects of the puzzle, and you can start the next step while they manage the completed one.

Whatever you decide, consider also what you want from it now and what you want to do with your free time. You can continue to work the project, you can start a business, you can expand into your next product, or you can let it run and play for a while. Examine this compared to the lifestyle you want. Then it's time to start the goals again. Tick off what was completed, and write new ones so that you always know where you are going.

Overall, keep putting in the strategies tighter, working your plan, educating yourself, investing in your product, company, and yourself, making sure you pick a mentor (I would love for you to consider me), and attending shows so you can keep up with what is going on in your industry.

Congratulations on taking the steps necessary to achieve your goals and to decide that you are going to work at it until you get what you want. You're worth it. I'm here to help. Many others are available to help and it is one of the few industries that would actually help their own competitor. If there is something you learn when you get here, there is more than enough for everyone.

CHAPTER 7 ACTION PLAN

- Get statistic tracking habits in place.
- Decide on your back end.
- Create your funnel from that.
- Create an ATM machine model.
- Be the Maker of Your Miracles.

What's Next?

By now you have either read the book and have a good feel for what you need to do and will start again and actually *do* the steps; or, you have done the steps and are ready to keep testing and tweaking and adding traffic, products, and improvements.

Before you continue, though, I want you to add one more step to your list: Visit www.Just31Days.com and get free tickets to live events I am speaking at, gifts for being a part of my community, videos that will highlight more, and continued tips, tricks, and trends of the trade.

I look forward to continuing to provide you with the Internet and social media information you need to grow your business, get your message out to the world, and create the freedom lifestyle you have always dreamed of.

Enjoy the journey.

About the Author

Top *Woman Speaker in the World for Internet Marketing.*

Tracy Repchuk's credentials include best-selling author, award-winning entrepreneur, winner of the New Internet Marketer of the Year 2007, the Stevie Award Finalist for Woman of the Year 2009, Coach of the Year Finalist for 2010, Coaching Institute, and International Woman's Day Leader Year 2008. She has appeared on ABC, NBC, CW, 7, King5, *USA Today*, 4 On Your Side, HGTV, and WBZ, has written countless articles for magazines, and appeared in newspaper articles, interviews, and two feature-length motivational movies.

Tracy is an international speaker and motivator, and has spoken in more than 27 countries in the past five years. She has appeared on the world's largest stages with many of the top speakers in the world.

Tracy graduated from Sheridan College at the age of 19 in 1985, and started her first business directly out of college.

While she operated her company she went to McMaster University for business, then transferred and completed her Certified Management Accountants designation. She has been self-employed ever since. During her multiple business ventures—which all still run today—she mastered many skills, including web design, direct sales copy writing, management, organization, strategic thinking, and Internet marketing.

Tracy has been deemed a "Quantum Leap Specialist," which means that she gets things done fast. Within eight months, Tracy had catapulted onto the scene earning six figures in six months. With her first book, which went from start to write it to best seller in 58 days, she won the 2007 New Internet Marketing Success of the Year award and was flown, all expenses paid, to Singapore to present her story to more than 3,400 attendees.

Tracy is a coach/mentor and consultant for Internet marketing and social media strategies, where she creates a cohesive solution across your entire business and online platform. This is her second book, and 23rd time published. Tracy is married to David Repchuk, her business partner of more than 19 years. They have three children—all are entrepreneurs.

www.TracyRepchuk.com